BRITAIN BETWEEN EAST AND WEST

Britain between East and West

A Concerned Independence

JOHN BURTON
Director,
Centre for the Analysis of Conflict,
University of Kent at Canterbury

A. J. R. GROOM
Centre for the Analysis of Conflict
and
Reader in International Relations,
University of Kent at Canterbury

C. R. MITCHELL
Centre for the Analysis of Conflict,
University of Kent at Canterbury
and
Senior Lecturer in International
Relations, The City University,
London

MARGOT LIGHT
Centre for the Analysis of Conflict,
University of Kent at Canterbury
and
Lecturer, Department of Linguistic
and International Studies,
University of Surrey

DENNIS J. D. SANDOLE
Centre for the Analysis of Conflict,
University of Kent at Canterbury
and
Associate Professor in Public Affairs,
George Mason University,
Fairfax, Virginia, U.S.A.

A Centre for the Analysis of Conflict Publication

Gower

Published by
Gower Publishing Company Limited,
Gower House, Croft Road, Aldershot, Hampshire GU11 3HR,
England

and

Gower Publishing Company,
Old Post Road, Brookfield, Vermont 05036, U.S.A.

British Library Cataloguing in Publication Data

Britain between East and West.
  1. Great Britain——Foreign relations——1945-
  I. Burton, John, 19-- ——
  327.41   DA589.8

ISBN 0-566-00722-3

Printed in Great Britain by Biddles Ltd, Guildford, Surrey

Contents

PART II TRENDS IN IDEAS AND EXPERIENCE IN WESTERN
EUROPE AND THE THIRD WORLD

PART III THE ROLE OF THE THIRD PARTY

PART IV THE FUTURE

Contributors

JOHN BURTON

Dr. John Burton is Director of the Centre for the Analysis
of Conflict at the University of Kent at Canterbury.
He has published twelve books and many articles in the
area of conflict research and international relations.
Prior to his academic career he had extensive diplomatic
experience as Permanent Head of the Australian Foreign
Office.

A.J.R. GROOM

Dr. A.J.R. Groom is Reader in International Relations
at the University of Kent at Canterbury. He is author,
co-author or co-editor of eight books and forty articles
in the fields of conflict research, strategic studies,
international relations and international organisation.
He has lectured extensively in North America, continental
Europe, Africa, Asia and the Antipodes.

MARGOT LIGHT

Margot Light is a Lecturer in Russian and Soviet Studies at the University of Surrey. She has published articles on Soviet foreign policy and foreign policy analysis. Her research interests include Soviet International Relations Theory and Conflict Analysis.

C.R. MITCHELL

Dr. C.R. Mitchell currently teaches International Relations at The City University, London, where he is a Senior Lecturer and has previously taught at the Universities of Surrey and Southampton, University College London and the University of Southern California. He originally taught modern history in secondary schools. He has been Hon. Secretary of the Conflict Research Society and helped to produce a BBC 'Horizon' programme on simulating international crisis behaviour.

DENNIS J.D. SANDOLE

Dr. J.D.J. Sandole has taught at University College London, The City University, University of Southern California (German and British Programs), and is currently an Associate Professor at George Mason University in Fairfax, Virginia, USA, where he teaches courses in international relations and conflict management. He has published in determinants of conflict, paradigm shifts, and the professionalisation of conflict management.

CENTRE FOR THE ANALYSIS OF CONFLICT

The Centre for the Analysis of Conflict is based at the University of Kent at Canterbury. It is a non-profit making research institution with members in several Universities in Britain and abroad. It undertakes research in the field of conflict research and upon request acts as a facilitator in the search for a resolution of particular conflicts. All the contributors are members of the Centre and have been associated with such exercises.

The Centre has well established links with research institutes abroad including those in the United States and the Soviet Union.

Preface

This monograph has been written by five teachers of International Relations who share what they believe to be a widespread concern for Britain's security and the future of world society. It is intended to provoke discussions on British foreign policy and the possibilities of a creative and helpful role that Britain could play in the currently threatening world political, economic and strategic situation. We hope it will result in discussion, debate and controversy in the United Kingdom and also in Eastern and Western Europe and the United States of America.

We have been stimulated to write this monograph in part by the obvious and urgent need for some new initiative given the present danger of nuclear war, and in part by the inadequate reponses that have been triggered in Western Europe, especially in Britain, by this danger. Unilateral disarmament, withdrawal from the Common Market, the removal of United States missiles from British territory, are important but negative ideas: there has been so far only this negative reaction to the dangers Britain (and the world) faces. We hope, in this publication, to place these issues in a wider perspective and to offer an alternative and positive foreign policy that reflects the fears and concerns of those putting forward such proposals for change and, also, the fears and concerns of those who oppose them.

John Burton
A.J.R. Groom
Margot Light
C.R. Mitchell
Dennis J.D. Sandole

August, 1983.

Introduction

"Great Britain has lost an empire
and has not yet found a role."
Dean Acheson, 1963.

This is an analysis of a new role which Britain could play in its own interests and in those of the wider international community.

What we have in mind includes the active participation of a 'third party' or 'facilitator' of the kind with which we are familiar in the context of small-scale disputes of an economic or social nature within societies. We believe that such a role can be enacted in the wider international community by a government and that such a role is now vital to world society. It is apparent that there is, at present, little hope of effective arms control or disarmament. Every conflict within the spheres of influence of the great Powers presents potential danger of escalated war. Traditional mediation and negotiation processes are not effective, and accidents and unforeseen circumstances can lead to behaviour and policies not intended and not desired. In short, there are situational imperatives driving us towards catastrophe.

Our conclusion is, therefore, that it is equally imperative to discover how to resolve conflicts, large and small, by means other than the coercive processes of bargaining, threat and confrontation.

Britain may be one of the few middle Powers with the experience, the geographical location, the relationships with other states in the developed and the developing world and the logistic capabilities required to enact such a role. Britain traditionally acted as a balancer within the European balance of power. What we are putting forward are techniques or policies that are relevant to the nuclear age - a different and more relevant kind of 'balancing' role, that of 'third party' or 'facilitator'.

For such a role a high level of objectivity and independence is required. By this we do not mean independence narrowly defined as a struggle for the elimination of formal ties with Western Europe, the removal of United States bases or the unilateral destruction of defence capabilities, although some or all of these may finally be involved. Independence is a complicated notion and we take space to describe it in its many forms: non-alignment, neutrality, neutralism, interdependence. We hope to show that what we have in mind is in line with long-established trends in Western Europe. It is also consistent with the traditions of flexibility in British foreign policies designed to promote British interests by seeking to maintain a just and stable world society.

However, such a shift in policy has wide implications, both domestic and foreign. Domestic and foreign issues are closely related due to the openness of Britain's economic and social structures. We seek to call attention to these implications and to examine them.

This monograph has four sections. Part I deals with the current position in world society and the opportunities for Britain. Britain seems to be at a stage where a reorientation in policy is not only possible, but is also being demanded. (Chapter One). We explain why we believe that it is a matter of urgency for a country, such as Britain, to emerge as a third party to help alleviate East-West and North-South relationships. Other middle Powers might also be attracted to this approach as part of their foreign policies. (Chapter Two). We then outline the options that seem to be open to Britain - arguing finally that the 'third party' option is logical and relevant. (Chapter Three).

Part II deals with foreign policy trends in world society generally. First we take a long term and universal view: there are persistent trends, from narrowly based national-interest policies, to those that reflect an understanding that security is best achieved for separate countries by policies that are concerned with universal security; from policies of negative neutrality, designed to isolate the state from world affairs, to policies that employ independent action as a means of making a positive contribution to stable relationships. (Chapter Four). More specifically we describe trends that have more recently taken place in Western Europe (Chapter Five) and in the Third World (Chapter Six).

Part III is about the role of the 'third party'. We commence by arguing that the conventional approach of acquiring and deploying armaments will continue because of fear and the perceived need for defence. However, alongside and complementary to it there can be a 'second track' seeking to solve problems and, thereby, to reduce this need. (Chapter Seven). An important component of this second track is the enactment of the third party role by a middle Power, and we describe just what this is. (Chapter Eight).

In Part IV we examine the domestic and foreign policy implications of the enactment of such a role. (Chapter Nine). We consider a programme by which such a change in policy can be promoted and conclude with the notion of 'Concerned Independence'. (Chapter Ten).

This book has been written as a basis for discussion among concerned people, not only in Britain, but also in all countries affected by the dangers of nuclear war, including the two principal nuclear Powers. It is their future that is at stake no less than the future of peoples elsewhere: the book is directed toward the solution of their problems, not toward isolation from them.

PART I
THE CURRENT SITUATION

In this opening section the problem is defined – the conditions in Britain that make possible and likely a change in foreign policy orientation (Chapter One), the nature of the East-West confrontation, including the need for a third party to assist the nuclear Powers in redefining their relationships and in resolving their problems (Chapter Two) and the options which current circumstances present to Britain, ranging from the continuation of present strategies to the adoption of a problem solving role (Chapter Three).

1 The readiness of Britain for change

PATTERNS OF CHANGE

Britain appears to be approaching one of those relatively rare times in its history when major changes in both structure and policy are necessary and possible. Moulds are being broken not merely in domestic politics but in economic thinking and policy, in public attitudes and expectations, in social and regional structures and, perhaps most important, in the external environment within which domestically chosen decision makers must operate. Radical and searching reconsideration of the United Kingdom's external posture is a necessary contribution to the present debate about Britain up to the year 2000.

One of the most powerful and prevalent beliefs about social and political change in Britain is that it occurs gradually, slowly, incrementally and – apparently – imperceptibly. Reform rather than revolution is said to be the British way. There is truth in this view; but the process is more complex. Since the industrial revolution, social and political change has proceeded less in a smooth, gradual evolution than in a series of jerks for which the previous quiescent periods have often provided periods of preparation.

This version of social change in Britain — that it proceeds at two quite different paces and is characterised by periods of sudden acceleration — suggests that changing Britain is often a matter of patience, of waiting until new ideas have been devised, debated and accepted and until old ideas — and hence accepted structures and ways of operating — have been discredited or rendered obsolete by events. Then a rapid programme of change can be implemented. The 1906 Liberal Government brought in a major programme of change. During the Second World War Churchill's administration began to plan major changes in the post war world.

The last great wave of change experienced by this country was initiated by Clement Attlee's Labour Government of 1945-51. In that period the main lines of Britain's post Second World War strategies were laid down and a start made in implementing them. All governments since 1945, Labour and Conservative, have been the heirs of that Labour Government working within the framework and developing the implications of strategies initiated in the early post war years. In 1948 Indian independence ushered in the policy of decolonisation which, with the granting of independence to Zimbabwe, has virtually run its course with the exception of some highly significant anomolies such as the Falklands, Hong Kong and Gibraltar. The signing of the Brussels Treaty in the same year and of the North Atlantic Treaty in the following year established the main lines of Britain's defence posture to the present. The Labour Government's decision to continue with the development of Britain's own nuclear weapons programme, as well as research into nuclear power, led to the development of Britain's own deterrent presently represented by the Royal Navy's ageing quartet of Polaris submarines, by even more ancient bombers and their increasingly expensive proposed replacements. In the same period, Britain's first timorous steps towards Europe, represented by accession to the Brussels Treaty in 1948 and the Council of Europe in 1949, were taken, albeit reluctantly. This reluctance continued to mark Britain's increasingly serious attempts to become a part of a unified Western Europe, which culminated in Britain's accession to the European Communities under a Conservative Government in 1973 and its subsequent confirmation by a referendum held under a Labour Government.

Domestically, the structure of the welfare state was laid down using the Beveridge proposals as a guideline rather than a blueprint. The National Health Service was established in spite of strong opposition from doctors in general and the British Medical Association in particular. The Education service was reconstructed along the lines established by Rab Butler's 1944 Education Act, although the question of private education was avoided to remain a matter for continuous debate and inactivity. Town and country planning was initiated and a series of disastrous decisions about new housing were taken in the genuine belief that high rise flats and council estates were automatic improvements on Victorian slums.

These examples serve to underline the contention that, in a very fundamental way, British politics over the last three decades have been a working out of a set of ideas and principles which emerged during the war and were accepted in the immediate post war period. This acceptance was epitomised by the phrase "Butskellism" in the 1950s, but it continued into the 1960s and even under the Heath administration and its Labour successors of the 1970s. However, the main acceleration in the rate of change came in the late 1940s. Since then the direction has been constant, but the pace has slowed. Change has been incremental and pragmatic, as in the classical belief about British society and its inherent stability, rather than swift and relatively far reaching.

Apart from the gradual discarding of old ideas, the increasing obsolescence of social structures and practices and the development of fresh doctrines, one of the seemingly necessary conditions essential for the British to face up to the need for rapid, substantial change, are some trigger events; these jolt established patterns of thinking and attitudes, not merely in intellectual and political circles, but throughout the country as a whole. The combined effects of the Depression of the 1930s and of the Second World War were necessary before the Attlee reforms could be implemented. The destruction of the 1930s and early 1940s (destruction of quite different types, but having equally jolting effects on both pro and anti change elements in British society) pointed up shortcomings in the way British society had previously been organised. It provided the spur to the development of criticism and of alternative ideas and, most importantly, it rendered the normally conservative population ready for some major restructuring of the way things were done in Britain. The world had changed; so Britain was changed.

ACCELERATED CHANGE IN THE 1980s

There are good grounds for arguing that Britain may be approaching another period in which accelerated, rather than normal change patterns, become probable. Certainly the political consensus upon which politics of the post war era has been built appears to have broken down with the advent to power of the present Conservative Government. It articulated a tough policy of economic change and a willingness to abandon assumptions about the role of the state in managing both the economy and the social services which have underpinned the policies of successive Labour and Conservative Governments. Equally, the splits within the opposition Labour Party, the emergence of the Social Democrats, the growth of support for the Liberals, the development of strong regional nationalism and the revival of opposition to the whole conception of the welfare state, all indicate that as the agenda of political debate changes, so attitudes and the underlying notion of national interests change.

All of these signs indicate that Britain may well be coming to the end of a period of incremental change and preparing again to face the necessity of carrying out some major alterations to the fabric of the country, rebuilding rather than redecorating or renovating. The late 1980s are likely, therefore, to be another major turning point in British social and political life.

What are the conditions that are making it necessary for the people of this country to brace themselves for a further round of rapid and serious change and accept the late 1980s as a challenge and an opportunity to alter course? Firstly, the outside world, to which Britain is intimately connected, is undergoing a series of major changes that cannot help but have an impact upon Britain's position and the range of options open to the country in its external affairs. Many people would disagree about the range and most important items, but each list would probably include:

(a) A major deterioration in relations between the super Powers, which has brought to an end the era of slowly growing détente but military weakness, particularly as perceived by the United States, has led to a reversion to the "cold war" attitudes that had gradually been eroded during the 1960s and early 1970s. Whatever the reasons for this change – and observers variously cite US reactions to Soviet involvement in Africa and Afghanistan, the continuation of the arms race, left wing movements in Latin and Central America and the failure of the Western interpretation of the human rights agreements concluded under <u>detente</u> – the fact remains that relations between the Soviet Union and the USA are worse now than they have been for more than twenty years. Any British government has to face the conundrum of remaining closely identified with an increasing hard-line and intransigent USA policy, or of adopting some alternative line more in keeping with realities as perceived from this side of the Atlantic.

(b) A fundamental and long-term energy problem which is likely to act as a constraint on both economic growth and political strategy for the forseeable future. Apart from the obvious effect of limiting economic activity in the industrialised countries, the longer term effects of the transfer of economic power to energy producers means quite simply that any growth in real income in industrialised countries is likely to be transfered in part to energy producers through higher energy prices. This is likely to continue as long as industrialised countries fail to find adequate alternative sources of energy. So far, few governments appear to have taken this problem seriously, except by talking about contingency plans to secure the safety of oil supplies by the use of military force.

(c) Linked geographically to the energy crisis is the accelerated growth of anti-Westernism represented by what is usually called 'the Islamic revival', a movement which has to be seen in the context of both the energy crisis and the demand among poor primary producing countries for a New International Economic Order. In a world of finite resources, some strategy has to be worked out for living less wastefully and for feeding ourselves more rationally and economically both on a national and a global basis.

(d) A steady increase of political violence and instability which particularly affects the countries of the poor and agrarian South, and which has also had its effects on both the industrialised North and upon the socialist bloc. The instability in

7

Northern Ireland is echoed in such places as Corsica, the Basque areas of Spain, Belgium, Yugoslavia, Poland and Quebec. Wars and civil wars in the Third World are occurring with increasing frequency and intensity. A Hungarian scholar has recently pointed out that between 1945 and 1970, 93 'local wars' occurred throughout the world; by 1976 the total had risen to 120. Military coups in Latin America have occurred at the rate of two each year over the last decade.

(e) This instability has to be seen against a background of increasing militarisation of both the entire globe and particularly of the countries of the South.

(f) There is, also, the growing transnational inter-dependence of all regions of the world, an inter-dependence formalised by membership of common regional and functional organisations, by informal trading and exchange systems, and by both deliberate and accidental involvement in the political affairs of others.

Not only has Britain's external environment changed massively and profoundly over the last decade, so has its domestic structure. Commentators of widely different persuasions seem to be agreed on one thing: the structures and processes originally set up in the post war era are no longer appropriate for dealing with the new range of problems facing Britain throughout and beyond the 1980s. It is argued on the Left that this failure can be seen in Labour's complete inability during the 1960s and 1970s to alter the balance of wealth in the country and to create a more just and equal society. By contrast, the Right argues that the inappropriateness of post war strategies, tactics and attitudes can be seen in failure to control inflation, to improve Britain's lamentable economic growth record and to offer incentives to those who would 'create wealth'. Attention must be given to these issues, it is argued, before any discussion of redistribution is undertaken. At another level, the failures of regional planning, of regional devolution, of refurbishing inner cities, of providing a flexible and satisfactory education system on a countrywide basis and of parliamentary reform, contributed to the erosion of confidence in the bases of welfarism and to the election in 1979, and its subsequent re-election, of a Government committed to a firm alternative philosophy and programme.

If the failure to complete the old political agenda of domestic politics has led to a crisis of confidence in what are increasingly seen as ineffective conventional methods, the inclusion of new items on the political agenda have stretched belief in the effectiveness of consensual politics to near breaking point. There seems to be no solution within conventional thinking for the continuing conflict in Northern Ireland. Latent racism in Britain has become increasingly overt as a remaining vestige of Britain's responsibility for her imperial past has settled in Brixton and Southall. A generation of black Britons has grown up in a hostile society and in a declining economy which offers few attractive opportunities to young white working class products of state education and hardly any at all to black. The solution to Britain's economic ills represented by Britain's entry into EEC has turned out to be a killing cure that merely hastens the economy down a declining path and accelerates what has become known as the 'de-industrialisation' of the country. The final choice among the famous 'three circles' of Britain's external relations – Atlantic, Commonwealth and Europe – has not proved a success, at least from a short term economic view-point, yet no-one has raised the question whether the three circles really represented the real extent of choices offered to Britain's policy makers in the 1950s and 1960s.

THE TRIGGER

A trigger making the late 1980s an opportunity for the British to accelerate their rate of change and to make radical decisions about the future, is the present government. It was voted into power on a wave of rejection of old solutions and of the remnants of the "Butskellist" tradition. Post-Thatcher Britain appears likely to be a condition in which rapid change and reform is both (i) a realistic option, because of the activities of Mrs. Thatcher and the consequences of her monetarist and hard-line policies; and (ii) a politically acceptable line to follow, because of the changed attitudes brought about by these same activities.

It is possible to argue this basic case from two different sets of assumptions. The first is that the present government's policies are, in the long run, the correct ones, in the sense that while they may be painful they will reduce inflation permanently, so that genuine economic

9

growth of something over the conventional 1.8% per annum of the post war years becomes a real possibility. In this positive scenario, the late 1980s will see a new, lean, efficient British industry backed by North Sea oil revenues and unencumbered by a militant workforce and powerful unions. It will be ready to serve as a platform on which to launch Britain's economic recovery and from which to confront the rest of the world with new confidence. The question will then arise as to how to use this opportunity both domestically and internationally. How will a Britain, redeemed by Thatcherism and monetarist doctrine, face the world of the late 1980s and the 1990s? What new ideas will assist Britain in such a refurbished condition to find a role in world affairs? How can such ideas be generated and debated?

The alternative, malign scenario, points equally to the late 1980s as a time when the British will have to confront the necessity for major changes and will probably be in the frame of mind to push them through. This view of the short term future involves a conviction that the Thatcher Government's policies are both totally wrong, in that they will not achieve any of their stated goals, and utterly disastrous, whether 'successful' or not, in having other effects on British economic, social and political life. In this scenario, large areas of the traditional British economy will be devastated, new industrial ventures will have been unable to start up through lack of investment or will have collapsed from overseas competition; unemployment will remain between three and four million and the only general growth points will be industries related to defence spending and the maintenance of law and order. This scenario is something like that painted by a 'round robin' of anti-monetarist economists to the Prime Minister. While 364 economists are not necessarily right, this does not mean that the monetarists still supporting the government are right either. If the first scenario is called 'a regenerated Britain', the second might be called 'a prostrate Britain'.

Whichever scenario is believed, Britain will be ready, indeed forced, to undertake a programme of accelerated change towards the end of the 1980s.

As we point out above, one of the preconditions for the British to undertake the task of major reform appears to be a general recognition that all is not well. While not arguing that the effects of the 1980's depression are likely to be as profound as those of the 1930's depression and the Second World War combined, nonetheless it seems undoubtedly the case that Britain is presently in the worst slump since the 1930s. The unemployment level has reached new records for the post war era and unemployment is affecting classes and categories previously immune from the problems of not having a job or income. The bankruptcy rate for business is also setting new records. If disaster is required to make the British as a whole more receptive to the idea of change and more willing to undertake the effort of reform, then the period since the summer of 1979 seems likely to have just such an effect. On the other hand, Mrs. Thatcher's re-election can be seen, at least in part, as a mandate for change. One of the results, then, of the present economic conditions, government policies whether they succeed or not and their social consequences, will be a mood in the country as a whole which will firstly stimulate the search for alternatives and then produce a political atmosphere in which major changes in all fields can be made. By the late 1980s a consensus for change is likely to exist in Britain. There is, however, likely to be little consensus about what that change should be.

DIMENSIONS OF THE DEBATE: INTERNAL AND EXTERNAL

The first stage in preparing a country for change is the launching of a full and frank debate to sort out options, objectives and strategies. This debate should look clearly and closely at Britain's medium and long term options and avoid the kind of short term ad hocery that too often characterised the political discussions of the 1960s and 1970s. If the post war consensus has broken down, then the least that can be done is to try to construct a new one, one that will be suitable for a Britain that is possibly post-industrial, post-homogeneous, post-Atlanticist and post-Imperial. We need to discuss not merely 'Where do we go from here?', but the nature of the domestic society we wish to aim at in the British Isles, and the type of role we believe Britain should try to play in its own interests in a world of post-détente international politics.

Given the nature of the external environment facing Britain and given the growing level of international and transnational interdependence, any debate on accelerated change for the country in the late 1980s must necessarily emphasise Britain's relationships with the outside world. This is partly because of the traditional openness, politically and economically, of the country to the international system. It is, also, because the kind of Britain we develop internally is highly dependent upon Britain's posture and behaviour externally. Relations with Third World primary producers and steel refiners vitally affect the structure of Britain's internal economy in a way that is likely to make attempts at economic autarky or isolation self-defeating in a very short time. Recent efforts to defend British textiles from Indonesian imports caused a loss to British high technology firms of large export orders to Indonesia.

Hence, a good starting point for any debate about future change in Britain is new options for the country's external posture and behaviour. Decisions in this field will automatically affect consideration of domestic options. How the British see their role in the world - as a full member of a more integrated EEC, as an isolated developing country protecting its declining or infant industries, as an adjunct to the USA or any other - profoundly affects the kind of domestic British society that will develop from the present crisis and the direction taken by the accelerated change that we anticipate.

BRITAIN'S FUTURE ROLE

Not only must Britain's relations with the rest of the world be discussed as a first step rather than as an afterthought, they must be discussed as a whole. It is true that the challenges to creative thinking posed by Britain's current international position are many and varied. They range from questions of security and political alignment to economic interdependence and the changing balance of economic influence within the global economic system. A major debate on this topic has already begun, but it has begun in a sporadic and patchy fashion, with a number of issues beginning to rouse considerable interest among intellectuals, political organisations, research centres and the public in general, while others are only just appearing on the agenda for national debate.

We would argue that it is essential to avoid the mistake of responding in a piecemeal fashion to a list of foreign policy challenges. A coherent framework or set of principles from which to operate is needed in order to formulate a coherent and appropriate posture towards the external environment of the late Twentieth and early Twenty-First Centuries, an environment which will be characterised by problems very different from those that existed in the post war world or even in the 1970s.

While Britain's interests, especially security interests, are our main concern, we are aware that British interests are inextricably linked to world interests and the international community interest. Britain is no longer a 'Power' that can determine the behaviour of others, but Britain still has influence that can persuade and help others. It can adopt, in its own interests, a concerned and positive interest in world affairs, a concern that in an interdependent world, other people's problems are necessarily our problems. There is no escape so that world society interests and British interests are one and the same thing.

Our main purpose is, therefore, to launch a discussion which will focus on the basic nature of British interests as these have become, and are likely to remain, in a complex, rapidly changing international environment. We seek to offer the principles for a rational future policy which will maximise those interests over a longer period than that represented by immediate advantage.

We can summarise these principles as a posture of greater independence. We advocate an independent, even a third party role for Britain. Independence is a word that has a number of conventional meanings and many connotations, but its meaning in terms of Britain's place in international politics should become clear as we spell out the third party role with which we associate it. At this point it is appropriate only to comment that the term 'concerned independence' was chosen because of its more positive connotations than 'non-alignment' or even 'positive neutralism'. It indicates an independent role that involves a basis for external relations that frees Britain from the constraints of various forms of dependency while ensuring the adoption of a positive and active role in the international system. It does not signify a retirement into isolation and protectionism.

2 The world situation

In the Introduction we claimed that traditional foreign and strategic policies are no longer relevant for a middle Power such as Britain. We have argued that there is a need, indeed an urgent need, for Britain (and others in a similar situation), in its own interests and in the interests of world society, to enact an independent third party role. The world system has managed to get along up to now with traditional deterrence strategies, power balances and international institutions designed to settle disputes and to prevent them leading to war. What has changed?

This question needs to be answered because it has always been widely accepted in Western political thought that violence, including warfare, is, in the last resort, a legal and legitimate means of bringing about change or preserving the existing order. It has been assumed that power balances, and deterrent strategies and institutions for collective security, serve to decrease the incidence of violence and of war. The Charter of the United Nations, drafted by persons who had been brought up in this tradition and before the full impact of warfare was understood, provides for the right of self-defence against aggression. Since neither self-defence nor aggression can be defined, states are still able to employ what power is at their disposal to pursue their interests.

Although deterrence strategies are supposed to prevent war, in practice, states have not relied upon them to do this. War has been traditionally an acceptable risk and a bearable cost to states seeking to control the international system. It seemed to be a rational means of maintaining order between 1480 and 1941 during which time there were 200 major 'world' wars. It is difficult for us today to accept war as an acceptable institution in international politics because we have a quite different conception of war and its costs.

Whatever the justifications in the past of war as an instrument of policy, clearly there is a need now for a changed system of control. In a nuclear world, war cannot be regarded as an acceptable means of controlling the international system. It has to be prevented. The uncertainties and risks of deterrence strategies cannot be entertained, even though the risks are regarded as low. They are, in fact, not low, as we shall try to show by analysing the nature of deterrence. Deterrence, power balancing by alliances, bargaining and negotiation, are no longer bearable means of maintaining order in international society.

There is, consequently, a crisis in political thought and in policy. A seemingly universal and rational philosophy and the politics based on it, appear now to be dangerous. This has happened so quickly, within the lifetime of one generation, that policy makers cannot come to grips with this reality. They still tend to operate in the traditional framework to which they can see no alternative. Where do we go from here?

THE CONTEMPORARY WORLD SITUATION

It is helpful to stand back and look at the situation that confronts us, especially the East-West relationship. What are the fears, what are the dangers? We are still not clear about what led to the Second World War. Why did the West continue to deny Germany and Japan access to raw materials and markets? Why did the war have to be fought when it resulted in giving both states what they had been demanding, thus making them, in effect, the winners? Was this to control the international system? What was the threat that was being avoided? So, too, in the present situation, what is the confrontation about? Does the United States wish to invade the Soviet Union or the other way around? Is a confrontation between two different political systems necessarily win-lose or are there possible changes over time that make this confrontation irrelevant? Are the changes promoted or impeded by confrontation? These questions are not usually discussed because the East-West relationship is defined in simple confrontation terms. Yet it is far from certain that East-West tension and conflict is, as popularly thought, a function of ideological differences. An alternative explanation may be that the significant source of tension between great Powers may be their greatness and, in particular, their relative stages of growth to greatness. All great Powers seem to have, or to have had a propensity for expansion as a necessary part of their great Power status whether in industry, trade, communication or diplomacy. The United Kingdom, the United States and the Soviet Union have each gone through stages of growth that altered the relative pecking order in international relations. Presumably China and other Powers will also grow. It is not difficult to hypothesize a systemic process: changes in technologies, environmental conditions and political and economic structures, lead to uneven rates of development giving opportunities to lesser Powers to catch up to greater Powers in industrial output and political influence. To begin with there is a struggle for parity so that there can be equal participation and an absence of domination. This struggle, for many reasons that are both psychological and systemic, becomes a struggle for superiority. There seems to be no way to call a halt. In the growth of industry, of social and political organizations, as well as of arms production, there is ample evidence that technical capabilities are used to the full, despite possible adverse consequences. What can be done, it seems, must be done.

At the international level a sphere of influence acquired by a state which is growing in power, needs to be protected by extensions beyond the boundaries of this sphere. If the Power has the capability, the sphere of influence will be so protected in this expansionist way. Then these extensions require protection, until there are 'foreign bases' scattered far from the national boundaries. Like all expansion processes, this one has inbuilt limits. Each extension is more costly than the last. There is a factor of distance; but more important in the modern world, there is the factor of political resistance in the penetrated regions. Once a state goes beyond what world opinion regards as 'legitimate' security needs, political resistances are generated abroad. In due course there is, also, competition between the resources needed for expansion – armed forces, subsidies and foreign expenditures – and resources needed for the satisfaction of consumer expectations. This competition gives rise to domestic resistance which can be suppressed only for a limited time. Finally, these foreign and domestic pressures make contraction essential in the foreign field. The United Kingdom seems to have gone through such a process. Recent American experience ₣ appears to be similar: post war expansionism, Vietnam, domestic unrest and foreign pressures, contraction associated with increased defence expenditure due to a perceived weakened status and, currently, a strong stand in this case in Central America. The tensions in East-West relations may be caused by these systemic processes in international relations which relate to growth and which have very little to do with types of political systems and ideologies.

Whether such processes operate or not, it is clear that states advancing in greatness use their influence to alter the international system and to adapt it to their interests, while relatively declining Powers seek to retain existing structures, spheres of interest and linkages. As a consequence, there are and always must be at any one time, 'revisionist' and 'status quo' Powers. Are East and West, the USA, the Soviet Union and China, accusing each other of essentially the same behaviour, that is, the behaviour of great Powers, the behaviour to be expected of states becoming powerful at relatively different rates, the behaviour associated with different stages of influence?

As part of this power political struggle there are, especially in our present post-imperial world, local struggles which great Powers use to promote their spheres of influence: Vietnam, Laos, Cambodia, Cuba, Angola, Ethiopia, Afghanistan, Philippines, Salvador, to mention only a few. In the post-imperial world in which there are many newly independent states, there are many internal liberation movements and attempts to change from oppressive, sometimes corrupt, regimes to ones that are legitimized.

Sometimes the Soviet Union is invited, or has the opportunity, to support these. In the normal course of events these liberation movements would bring about change, sometimes gradually, sometimes by local violence, without external intervention. While the West could probably accept political change by indigenous processes, for strategic reasons it must oppose liberation movements that have Soviet support. The result often is that while the USSR is seen to support liberation movements, the West currently seems to defend regimes in many areas of the world that could not survive without external support. Each side in this power struggle, however, perceives the behaviour of the other, not as the systemic and inevitable consequence of their own power struggle, but as an intended deliberate threat to the other. While in the latter case there is good reason for fear and defence, in the former case there is good reason for co-operative efforts in overcoming the systemic processes.

While the Soviet Union has the advantage that it tends to be invited to support movements against non-legitimized authorities, it is in a strategically disadvantagous position because of the unbalanced spheres of interest which existed before it became a major Power. Until the mid 1970s, the USA had virtually the whole globe, apart from the Soviet Union and its immediate neighbours, as its sphere of influence and location for bases. The Soviet Union perceived the threat of political intervention within its own immediate region in addition to the more general nuclear threat that both share.

Whether they support one type of regime or another, both sides have found that paradoxically they lose control over their client states once they give support. The USA pressed the Saigon Government to modify its policies and widen the political base of its support; but Saigon knew that it was strategically important to the USA and did not have to modify its oppressive policies. Several other governments currently are inflexible in their policies knowing that the USA is in the last resort committed to them. This is a general situation in the Western sphere of influence, leading to wide-spread instability. A similar situation occurs in the Soviet sphere. A revolt in Ethiopia led to one repressive regime taking over from another. In Afghanistan, where political stability was important to the Soviet Union in view of events in Iran, the early Soviet sponsored regime was deaf to pleas for policies that would broaden its political base. Thus, the rivalry between the great Powers has consequences throughout world society, creating increasing instability and situations that cause serious tensions, crises and wars. The major Powers cannot control the consequences of their power rivalries.

Underlying the power confrontation there are serious domestic problems on both sides. As observed above, imperialisms appear to crumble once they over extend their spheres of interest, and once costs escalate to the point at which the middle class suffers and the internal infrastructures are weakened. Both the USA and the Soviet Union are feeling the effects of their expansionisms. In addition, both have their own sources of internal dissent and disintegration within their spheres of influence. However, in a bilateral power struggle the result is not a progressive withdrawal on the British model. The internal consequences are readily blamed on the other side and, faced with internal defeat and therefore with nothing to lose, one side or the other is likely to try to solve its internal problems by promoting the perception of external threats and by external interventions.

In sum, the world situation is currently one in which the great Powers are locked into a confrontation which they cannot themselves control. There are processes operating which are harmful to both that are, nevertheless, inherent in the power politics approach which both adopt. Neither can give way because this would be interpreted as weakness. Each pursues superiority while both rely on deterrence.

THE FALLACY OF DETERRENCE

In this context let us go back to the question whether mutual deterrence can ever be a reliable instrument. Deterrence strategies are the main means by which the major Powers endeavour to control their power rivalries. However, the fact of many past wars indicates that deterrence is not an effective instrument. Indeed, it may be that deterrence has built into it processes of escalation that render it self-defeating. The reasons why deterrence fails are now becoming clearer.

Threat of punishment, threat of costs greater than satisfactions to be gained, has an influence on the decisions of individuals and groups. The rules of the road, parking rules, are obeyed in many cases because of threat. However, often a deliberate costing is undergone and sometimes there is a calculated preference for a fine that is less costly than the gains to be made from defiance of the law in particular circumstances. It may be that some crimes are deterred by the threat of costs greater than any possible gains, but we cannot assume that societies are as harmonious as they are because of threats and deterrents. Coercion may not be the explanation of social order.

At first thought the assumption that deterrence deters seems axiomatic. Its validity is fundamental to our notions of social organisation and law and order. When in practice threats fail to deter, it is usually argued that this is merely because the amount of deterrence and coercion, and the risk of detection, are less than required, or that some different form of deterrence and detection is needed. No other explanation of the failure of coercion to contain 'unlawful' behaviour is possible within the framework of traditional views. To recognize the failure of deterrence as an instrument of control would jeopardize a whole set of conventional notions involving rights, obligations, morality, values, the socialisation process and the justice of institutions and legal processes.

The assumption that deterrence deters is so taken for granted that writers have concentrated mainly on its processes, for example, how threats can be made more effective by ensuring credibility, by promoting accurate perceptions of the threat and by maintaining a sensible relationship between crime and punishment. Other studies focus on the relationship between levels of punishment and degrees of risk of being apprehended. Rarely is the effectiveness of deterrence seriously questioned. Yet the empirical evidence of crime statistics and wars suggests strongly that deterrence does not always deter.

The assumption that deterrence deters is clearly articulated at the strategic level. National defence strategy is merely a special case of the belief that adequate negative sanctions prevent the 'rational' decision maker from being 'aggressive'. NATO officials argue that if it had not been for NATO there would have been aggression in Europe from the East. Warsaw Pact officials probably use a similar argument. 'How do you know?' is regarded as an irrelevant or unnecessary question. After all, there has been no European war since 1945.

But there may not have been one anyway had there been no NATO. In practice, whether such deterrence deters cannot be established because there cannot be a test. We can only demonstrate when deterrence fails not when it 'succeeds' for its success may be due to many other factors and cannot be attributed solely or mainly to the particular threat. We must reason out an answer – and such reasoning does not support the belief that deterrence is an effective control measure.

In the pre-nuclear age there was strong empirical evidence that strategic balances and military threats did not always deter 'aggression'. They may have in some cases, we do not know. There is no evidence that the nuclear threat is any more of a deterrent than was the mighty power of the United States against Japan when the latter bombed Pearl Harbour. The failure of capital punishment to deter those engaged in organised fighting and killing in a communal conflict would suggest that in some circumstances 'rational behaviour' includes the acceptance of the risk of paying the highest possible price – which means that there is no deterrent. On these purely formal and logical grounds the assumption needs to be questioned whether deterrence is, in any but the most trivial circumstances, an effective mechanism of control.

On an inter-personal level behaviour is effectively controlled, not because of coercion by authorities to observe legal norms, but because a value is attached to relationships which would be threatened by antisocial (legal and non-legal) behaviour. It follows that if circumstances occur which deny to the actor in any area of his behaviour the opportunity to interact, there are decreased incentives to conform in addition to decreased opportunities even to know what is required of him in that area of behaviour. It may be that threat and deterrence are subject to limited boundaries of effectiveness, being relevant only in relation to the daily rules of social relationships that rest on mutual convenience, such as rules of the road. It may be that they have only marginal relevance for behaviour which can destroy social harmony, for example, violence against the person, corruption, exploitation, robbery and revolt. The degree of social harmony enjoyed by societies may be due to different influences, such as values attached to satisfactory transactional relationships. If this is indeed the case, quite fundamental changes are required in the policies designed to promote harmonious social relationships. Even in the most ideal social system there is a measure of disharmony due to structural and institutional constraints on behaviour. Unless attention is given to the values attached to relationships, it is likely that deviant behaviour may be more pronounced than it need be. The punishment of deviance is likely to increase it rather than to decrease it.

The same reasoning can be applied to the inter-states level. In a great Power rivalry the tendency is to isolate, to withdraw recognition, to resist parity, to withhold technology and needed supplies as a threat or punishment. As was the case for Japan in the 1930s, ultimately there is nothing to be gained and everything to be lost by observing the norms of international society if these threaten some important national interests. Similarly the ending of 'detente' with its positive advantages for all, undermines any influences imposed by deterrent strategies. If the Soviet Union or the United States are seen to be experiencing internal problems that take time to resolve or problems in their spheres of interest, this requires co-operative and not threatening responses, otherwise power rivalries will lead to war.

THE FALLACY OF NEGOTIATION

A study group was set up in 1963 by the David Davies Memorial Institute for International Studies to examine the peaceful settlement of international disputes. Its membership ensured a serious and thoughtful analysis. The views expressed represented conventional wisdom and informed opinion on this subject. The striking feature of the report was the way in which the group was pulled in two different directions. On the one hand confidence in judicial processes was affirmed and reaffirmed; on the other, there was a realistic acknowledgement that they had failed.

The study group argued that there was nothing funda-mentally inadequate in judicial procedures; the problem was a lack of willingness on the part of states to submit to voluntary or compulsory third party determinations. This begs the main question: if states are unwilling to adopt judicial and formal procedures that take decision making away from them, then these procedures are irrelevant to the circumstances. It is of no avail to bemoan the condition of world society and blame states for the lack of success of some techniques. The intellectual difficulties experienced in re-thinking traditional means of peaceful settlement of disputes cannot be overcome by impressing upon states their moral obligation to fall in with behavioural patterns suggested by intellectuals and idealists. The reality is that both judicial procedures and the less formal processes of mediation are incompatible with the nature and operations of international and, indeed, with many aspects of municipal, society.

Techniques for the resolution of conflict need to reflect the felt needs of those concerned. Procedures that postulate conflict as a situation in which the gain of one party is the loss of the other, cannot lead to a decision that satisfies all parties. Judicial processes are of this kind. Arbitration and conciliation and, indeed, even more informal procedures such as bilateral bargaining and negotiation, assume that bargains and compromises are desirable and possible and that external pressures can help to make them stick. Studies of human behaviour suggest that this assumption is wrong. The independent decision making role of states in world society is more jealously defended than in most other relationships. The techniques fail because their objective is settlement by third party decision making or by compromises that do not fully and equitably satisfy the needs and aspirations of all parties. Traditional techniques of bargaining and negotiation lack a problem solving dimension.

THE ALTERNATIVE TO CONTROL BY POWER

If there is a tendency for states to expand and to employ their resources to protect their spheres of influence, if threat and deterrence do not constrain and if bargaining and negotiation are not effective means of arriving at mutual agreements, what are the alternatives?

In an ideal world the alternative would be to create relationships that are so valued that constraints are self-imposed. Indeed, this was the remedy of nineteenth century laissez-faire economists who thought that the market mechanism would promote mutual interests in interdependence. This was a worthy goal. However, the creation of valued relationships is more difficult. In any event there cannot be such a free-market economy.

One other ideal solution could be for all middle and smaller Powers to adopt neutral postures and thus to isolate the nuclear Powers, forcing these major rivals to face each other directly in a mutual deterrence situation, with no opportunity for making use of other states or for intervening in their affairs. Spheres of influence would then be eliminated. Again, this could be a worthy objective, but the means towards it are too remote and long term to be interesting.

What we are seeking in a nuclear world is the resolution of conflicts by non-power processes, by processes that do not include alliances and threats or even power bargaining and negotiation. What these processes are in practice and in their practical application is discussed later: all that we wish to argue at this stage is that there is an urgent need to avoid reliance on deterrent strategies, and an urgent need for non-power processes to be initiated by a relevant state or states enacting a third party role.

Britain could be that relevant state. Britain has had a long experience acting as a controller in a power system. It has exercised influence and control by military power-balancing, as an imperial Power and in a trading role. This type of behaviour is no longer relevant. In any event, Britain is no longer in a position to act in this way. Even through association with other European states it cannot enact this controlling role. They have diverse interests. Furthermore, in the world society of today with some 170 states, no such nineteenth century control is possible, no matter what the power.

At the same time and as a result of its past role, Britain still has links and associations throughout world society that are mutually valued, yet under-utilized. Many are institutionalised through the Commonwealth, many are preserved by culture and historic memory. They are there to be put to good use in the pursuit of less immediately self-interested, and more world society oriented goals. They give Britain entry into both East-West and North-South relationships.

In respect of East-West relations, Britain as a former great Power, having experienced the stages of growth and decline, is in a strong position to place ideological and other differences in a broader perspective and to facilitate communications and greater analytical understanding between the contemporary great Powers. Its long and wide connections with the developing world enable it to present an authoritative picture of the problems and prospects in North-South relations. So far it has failed to do so and to capitalise upon its assets. It has not yet rid itself of its power and alliance traditions and its imperialistic attitudes.

It is for this reason that a note of warning needs to be sounded about the nature of the independent third party role we have in mind and which we spell out in later Chapters. Recently, Britain has been widely credited with positive achievements in relation to the Rhodesian-Zimbabwe settlement. This is a mistake. A constitutional settlement that did not take into account ethnic rivalries had to lead to conflict. Noting this mistake serves to clarify the distinction we wish to make between a former controlling role within a coercive framework and the constructive third party role that is relevant to contemporary world society.

Britain's record in decolonisation is not a good one. While credit must be given for its smooth and largely non-violent withdrawal from imperialism, little credit should be given for the type of independence granted and the consequent conflicts. The communal problems of India were clear before independence was granted and little attempt was made to adjust the constitution or the processes of independence to the known conditions. The assumption that a state could be made of peoples controlled and organised within boundaries determined by an imperial Power was a false one. Conflict resulted. The same story was repeated time after time – Palestine, Cyprus, Nigeria, Malaya and others. There were imposed constitutional settlements, usually with minimal consultation with the parties concerned and with little regard to ethnic and tribal conflicts.

The Rhodesian-Zimbabwe settlement followed this pattern. The various factions were invited to a constitutional conference. They were presented with a draft. Their immediate reaction was to suggest that before a constitution was discussed, the problems existing in their ethnic and other relationships should be discussed. Perhaps more than one state would be desirable, perhaps a developed state. Only then should a constitution be drafted and negotiated. However, they were firmly told that they had been invited to a constitutional conference. They could suggest amendments, but that was that. So it is with Northern Ireland where attempts have been made to impose a constitutional settlement. Britain has acted in a benevolent and paternalistic way, but with a view to enforcing settlements, not solving the basic problems. The trend continues in the post-repossession policy over the Falklands.

It is this experience of failure in imposing settlements, in coercive bargaining and negotiation, which should force Britain to question the assumptions, values and philosophies it has traditionally followed and which are still those of the great Powers. It is this failure which could enable Britain to explore means of resolving conflicts outside the coercive framework which Britain itself has helped to create and to institutionalise.

3 British options in the 1980s and beyond

INTRODUCTION

Since domestic as well as international events and trends
have made it highly likely that Britain will undergo
radical change during the 1980s, what are some of the
foreign policy options which Britain could pursue in
the 1980s and beyond?

BRITAIN'S EXTERNAL RELATIONSHIPS

In the period since the end of the Second World War,
Britain has been undergoing general decline as a world
Power. During the long life of its Empire it was a
world Power of first rank – supervising the maintenance
of the balance of power in Europe, as well as expanding
its colonial rule across six continents. However, with
post–Second World War economic crises, decolonisation
and reductions in military capability and commitments,
Britain no longer has this role.

Nevertheless, vestiges of Britain's imperial past remain.
For instance, it is still linked with those parts of
the world which comprised its Empire. The infrastructure

in terms of which Britain maintains this status with its former colonial areas is the Commonwealth – 'a voluntary association of states which have experienced some form of British rule who wish to work together to further their individual and common interests.' What is especially interesting about the Commonwealth is that, given that most of its members are part of the non-aligned, economically developing South, Britain has a ready-made connection with the less developed world.

Britain is, of course, historically located amongst the economically developed nations of the North. In this regard, it is a member of the Organisation for Economic Co-operation and Development (OECD) which is effectively the architect and maintainer of an international economic system which tends to benefit the North, to a large degree, willy-nilly, at the expense of the South. Thus the North, with a quarter of the world's population, has four-fifths of the world's income while the South, with three-quarters of the world's population, has a mere one-fifth of the world's income. In addition, there are a number of poor countries in the South which are faced with growing food deficits and possibly mass starvation. For instance, there are already in excess of 800 million people near starvation and their numbers are increasing. Further, money spent on official development aid amounts to less than 5% of the money spent by the world on armaments.

In the face of such a human catastrophe the British Government has even suggested that its foreign aid to developing countries should be cut by 15% up to 1984. Hence, though Britain's membership and unique historical status in the Commonwealth enables it, in principle, to act as a bridge between North and South, the Southern members of the Commonwealth may not feel that the potential of this bridge has yet been realised.

In its relationship with the Commonwealth, Britain has, in fact, tended to adopt a very low profile. Indeed, politically, the organisation is no longer 'British-led or even Anglo-centric', although it is difficult to imagine a Commonwealth without Britain. One of the reasons why Britain has assumed a lower posture with regard to the Commonwealth is its entry into the European Communities in 1973. Having come to the conclusion that it was becoming increasingly difficult to influence the United States alone and that it was not possible to turn the Commonwealth into a British-led force in international affairs, Britain went against its own historical tradition of maintaining some sense of distance between itself and continental Europe and applied for entry into the European Communities. It did so only in 1961, after having declined membership in the European Coal and Steel Community (ECSC) in 1951 and refusing to enter the European Economic Community in 1957. Partly because of its attitude to European integration, Britain's application resulted in two humiliating French-led rejections before entry was finally achieved in 1973.

As one of the world's largest and most powerful economic and political units, the European Communities represent an opportunity for Britain to achieve what it could not achieve with the Commonwealth or the United States - reassertion of its former status as a force in world affairs. However, for many in Britain, particularly those in the Labour Party and trade unions, membership in the Communities has stimulated, rather than undermined or even contained the forces making for Britain's economic and political decline. Many have even argued for withdrawal on the assumption that by cutting itself loose, Britain would be able to do more, not only for itself, but for the Commonwealth and, by implication, for the Third World in general.

Thus far, we have referred only to Britain's location along the North-South dimension and of its unique role as a bridge between those hemispheres. Britain is also located along the East-West dimension which currently displaces the North-South relationship as a source of international tensions. Moreover, Britain plays no bridging role here because it is firmly located in one hemisphere within that dimension - the West. In this regard, Britain was a signatory of the North Atlantic Treaty which was established in 1949 as a counter to a perceived Soviet threat to world peace. From a British/European viewpoint, NATO was also created to bind the United States to Europe's defence. Many recalled that the USA entered both World Wars two to three years after the Europeans became involved.

As a member of the Western Alliance, Britain maintains the British Army of the Rhine (BAOR) in West Germany, which includes a regiment of Lance tactical nuclear missiles. It has also provided about 70% of the NATO naval forces in the Eastern Atlantic and Channel areas. It allows the US to maintain military forces, including nuclear weapons, throughout the United Kingdom. There are some 105 US bases on British soil. In manpower terms, this amounts to about 27,000 USA military personnel and 31,000 dependents. In addition, as part of the NATO decision taken on 12 December 1979 to modernise 'theatre nuclear forces' (TNF) in Western Europe, Britain has consented to receive 160 US Cruise missiles by 1983-85. This decision which was taken, in part, to counter Soviet deployment of the SS-20 missile, will continue to fuel controversy and political activity in Britain as well as in the other countries, such as West Germany, Italy, Holland and Belgium, which are supposed to receive the new missiles.

The final ingredient of Britain's military alignment with the West is its membership in the nuclear club. It is one of five countries in the world known to possess operational intercontinental nuclear weapons. These are the five permanent members of the UN Security Council. Though the size of the British nuclear force is dwarfed by that of the USA and the USSR, its destructive potential is substantial even against defended targets and after withstanding a first strike. While the present force will see Britain through as a military nuclear Power until the end of this century, Britain will - through the implementation of the decision to replace Polaris with the longer-range (up to 6000 miles) more accurate USA Trident system, at a minimum cost of £5000 million over the next 15 years - remain a global nuclear Power well into the next century.

Britain has a special relationship with the USA, a relationship which is special in a specific as well as in a general sense. Britain and the United States are linked by virtue of a shared history, language and institutions. This general 'special' relationship accounts to some extent for the relationship in the specific sense, which concerns Britain's status as a nuclear Power. In this regard, though Britain produces its own submarines and nuclear warheads, America provides the missiles. It does this for no other country in the world. Though the nuclear special relationship initially involved reciprocity, it has come to mean growing British dependence upon the USA for full operational realisation of Britain's status as a nuclear Power, the case of Trident being the most recent example.

THE STATUS QUO OR CHANGE?

In these conditions, Britain has been attempting to find a post-imperial role or, more accurately, to find new ways of enacting a world role, so necessary for its security. It has attempted this through the Commonwealth and the EEC with regard to the North-South relationship and through NATO, a USA military presence and its own nuclear deterrent with regard to the East-West relationship. Nevertheless, Britain's economic, political and military decline has continued. This raises an obvious question: should Britain contemplate doing something other than what it has been doing for the last 35 years?

NORTH-SOUTH OPTIONS

Britain maintains a relatively low profile within the Commonwealth. Indeed, leadership has been assumed by Canada, Australia, Tanzania, Zambia and latterly India, as well as by the Commonwealth Secretariat. Though there are good reasons, in the sense of 'post-imperial ethics' why Britain should not, indeed, probably could not, re-establish itself as leader, it could nevertheless play a greater role within the Commonwealth.

To play such a role is to become more involved with the problems faced by the Southern members of the Commonwealth and, through them, with the problems confronting the Third World in general and in attempts to resolve the conflicts which are occurring along the North-South divide. Though East-West relations and the possibility of nuclear catastrophe are, in the short run, the greater sources of international tensions and, hence, command most of our attention, North-South relations pose the greater risks in the long run.

There are hard, practical as well as ethical reasons for this view. The countries of the South have organised themselves into groupings of various kinds, thereby moving in the direction of mobilizing their resources for expressing and pursuing their interests more effectively. Perhaps the most salient and influential of all southern groupings is the Organisation of Petroleum Exporting Countries (OPEC) which influences the supply and, therefore, the price of oil on the international market. More general 'southern' views are reflected by the Group of 77. Moreover, within the context of both the East-West and North-South relationship, many developing countries are members of the Non-aligned Movement.

The Non-aligned Movement invites an interesting response from Britain. All countries are involved in and are affected by East-West and North-South tensions, whether they belong to corresponding groupings or not. Moreover, the different sets of problems and conflicts do not occur independently of each other. The North-South can influence and exacerbate the East-West relationship and vice versa. Though this spill-over factor may complicate problem solving in either dimension, it also makes it more imperative that such problem solving be attempted. As already mentioned, Britain is already exceptionally well-placed to do this with regard to the North-South dimension.

However, in order to undertake such action, to play more effectively the role of a bridge between North and South, Britain will first have to help to open up the North, and especially the European Communities. Britain will necessarily be involved in the resolution of the fundamental structural problems that the Communities are now universally acknowledged to be facing, and it can bring a North-South, as well as British dimension, to their resolution in a similar manner to the way in which it has successfully looked after the special interests of New Zealand.

THE EAST-WEST OPTIONS

Since the 1979 NATO decision to base US Cruise and Pershing missiles in Europe, the European perception of a nuclear war taking place in and being confined to this continent, has received considerable reinforcement from rhetoric and actions associated with the Reagan Administration in Washington. Amongst these is the US decision to develop enhanced radiation warheads (ERW), the so-called 'neutron bomb', which is actually a low-yield hydrogen device. Because it is designed for short range battlefield use, particularly against tanks, and because it produces less heat and blast but more 'prompt' radiation than other nuclear weapons, ERW is seen by many as an American signal that nuclear war, particularly in Europe, is not only 'thinkable' but also 'do-able'. Put another way, a conventional war in Europe might escalate to a nuclear confrontation sooner rather than later. This notion has been strengthened by Alexander Haig's statement that NATO doctrine includes the possibility of firing a nuclear 'warning shot' to demonstrate to the Soviets that their behaviour has 'exceeded acceptable levels of toleration'. There was, also, President Reagan's comment that he could imagine a nuclear exchange taking place in Europe, without either super Power attacking the territory of the other.

All of this has fuelled the anxieties of concerned Europeans. In Britain, the Campaign for Nuclear Disarmament (CND) has revived after nearly 20 years of inactivity. And it is not only the revival of CND and similar organisations in other countries, but also a shift in public opinion in general which seems to be signalling to the British Government, among others, that it should be examining alternatives to its present defence position. This factor appears to be persisting despite the electoral successes of Herr Kohl and Mrs. Thatcher and is reflected in the opinion polls and the continuing support given to the protest organisations. This suggests that there is a substantial public sentiment in Britain for the reduction, if not the complete elimination, of its nuclear profile, both in terms of its own weapons but more especially in terms of those of the USA which are based on British soil.

There is evidently not at present a similar sentiment in regard to membership in NATO, although there are some clear options. One option would be for Britain to adopt the 'French Model', that is withdraw from NATO's integrated military structure but still remain within the Alliance. In this case, Britain would withdraw from the integrated command structure but retain its seat on NATO's governing body, the North Atlantic Council. Britain would also ask the United States to withdraw its bases both nuclear and conventional. It would retain its own nuclear forces. Another option would be for Britain to adopt the 'Norwegian Model', that is, following Norway and remain in NATO militarily as well as politically, but not allow the deployment of nuclear weapons or foreign troops except during times of crisis. This would mean negotiating the withdrawal of US bases, reversing the decision on Cruise and pursuing nuclear disarmament. A third option would be for Britain to adopt the 'Euro Model', that is withdraw completely from NATO and participate in the creation of some kind of Western

European security arrangement. Appropriate infrastructures already exist which could facilitate the development of some kind of Euro-security arrangement – the Western European Union (WEU) or the Independent European Programme Group (IEPG). A final option would be for Britain to adopt the 'Swedish/Swiss Model'. In this case, Britain would withdraw completely from NATO, refrain from participating in any subsequent military-alliance system, negotiate the withdrawal of USA bases, reverse its decision on Cruise missiles, pursue nuclear disarmament and maintain a strong conventional military capability. In effect, it would pursue the goal of armed neutrality associated with Sweden and Switzerland. These options could be seen as a progression. Britain could, for instance, opt first for the French position and then a modification of the Norwegian position, that is remain outside the integrated command structure, then opt for the Euro-position and, ultimately, move on to the Swedish/Swiss position. Though we have focussed our attention specifically on Britain, much of what we have said applies to other countries as well, especially those in Europe. We have already mentioned that the decision taken by NATO in December 1979 has caused a great deal of turmoil in those member-countries which are supposed to receive the new missiles.

CONCLUSION

Since 1945 the potential for global disruption, indeed holocaust, has reached mind-numbing proportions, primarily as a consequence of the conflicts which have developed along the North-South and East-West axes. During that time Britain has undergone progressive economic, political and military decline. The more it declined, the more it tended to place its bets on apparently sure things: the United States, NATO, the nuclear deterrent and Europe. Each of these 'sure things', however, has proved to be of variable or dubious reliability as a source of international influence; indeed, even as a source of political, military or economic security. Britain has not, therefore, found a really sure thing. It has not been able to put to rest, once and for all, that now classic but still uncomfortable comment made some 20 years ago by the then US Secretary of State, Dean Acheson, 'Britain has lost an Empire and has not yet found a role'.

It can even be argued that the particular attempts undertaken by Britain to retain its world role have not only been unsuccessful, but have also exacerbated North-South and East-West tensions. Britain has, after all, taken sides in each of the corresponding conflicts. As a member of the OECD and the European Communities it is obviously a member of the North, although its membership in the Commonwealth enables it to play, at least in principle, a bridging role between North and South. As a member of NATO, with US forces on its soil, and its own independent nuclear strike force targetted on the Soviet Union, it is obviously a member of the West.

Against this background, we have looked at some options which Britain could pursue, options which represent various degrees of independence from the firm alignments associated with North-South and East-West. As argued elsewhere in this volume, independence does not necessarily mean cutting ties and pursuing a policy of neutrality or isolationism. What it means is the avoidance or termination of <u>exclusive</u> alignments and ones that just promote narrow national interests. If Britain were able and willing to reduce the exclusivity of its associations with and commitments to North and West, it would be better placed to approach North-South and East-West conflicts, not as a partisan, but as a supportive third party intent on pursuing the resolution of those conflicts in a manner which was acceptable to the parties concerned. By pursuing such a problem solving policy, one which involved the promotion of the interests of others, Britain would effectively be promoting its own interests. In this regard, it would obviously be far easier to invest in one's own development if external tensions and threats were at a minimum than if they were escalating to the point of no return. If it succeeded in the promotion of its own and others' interests, Britain might well have succeeded in finding that long-elusive post-imperial role.

Accordingly, we advocate what we feel is the 'right direction' for Britain in the late 1980s and beyond, an independent role in world affairs. Given the public opinion and actions we have looked at, we are apparently not alone in our view.

PART II
TRENDS IN IDEAS AND EXPERIENCE IN WESTERN EUROPE AND THE THIRD WORLD

A positive third party role implies a high level of objectivity and independence. Such independence implies more than being neutral or non-aligned; yet neutrals and the non-aligned have little by little drawn nearer to such a positive role. Indeed, there is reason to believe that there has been and is a strong trend within the world system for states to regard independence and positive attitudes to world problems as the norm, although defensive alliance structures were regarded as the norm up until the Second World War. This reflects the political realities of the twentieth century – the realities of independence and interdependence in a nuclear environment.

We have thought it would be useful, therefore, to trace the history of these trends both in Western Europe and in the Third World. Some clarification of neutrality, neutralism, non-alignment and the other forms of independence help to show how a third party role – or a 'concerned independence' – is a further development along this same spectrum. One could argue, historically, that the emergence of a concerned independence or policies that seek to resolve international problems outside a power framework, will become the norm and that states that are slow to move in this direction will be doing both themselves and the wider world society a disservice that could be disastrous for both.

Chapter Four discusses the various concepts that are labelled 'independence' – from neutrality to non-alignment to 'concerned independence'. Then we outline Western European experience (Chapter Five) and the way in which countries in the Third World have gravitated toward an independence in foreign policies that is active and intended to make a positive contribution to their own security through international stability (Chapter Six).

4 Towards concerned independence

THE EVOLUTION OF SOVEREIGNTY

The range of foreign policy options which this Chapter
identifies has always been and will always be available.
However, in the minds of decision makers and publics
some of these options are deemed more relevant to the
particular times than others which are then not approached
with an open mind. So it is with the 'alignment' of
Britain with the United States. It is deemed right
for the times. By contrast many would not even contemplate
'concerned independence'. The authors of this book think
otherwise. We have come to this view after looking
at the options available to states, in an historically
evolutionary way. This historical evolution is not a
neat and tidy affair with one period beginning as the
previous one ends. On the contrary, there is overlapping:
old policies and ideas remain and still claim their
adherents and advocates. So it is that each of the options
discussed has and, perhaps, will always have, its champions
at any time. However, we feel that historical evolution,
the contemporary world situation and Britain's domestic
needs make a policy of concerned independence the most
appropriate foreign policy for Britain today.

In our view there is a continuity and evolution from
the sovereign independence of the state as it emerged
from the Middle Ages, to the concerned independence
which we see as appropriate in the contemporary world.
The difference between earlier notions of sovereignty
and concerned independence reflects a changed and much
more interdependent world; it reflects a reaction against
the self-centred pursuit of sovereign independence by
some states and its denial to others. Power politics
has led to economic disruption, world wars and the present
possibility of a nuclear war. Vulnerable states have
been induced to look to alliances, neutrality and other
palliatives to preserve their sovereign independence.
Recently, the newly-independent states have attempted
to safeguard their new status with a policy of non-
alignment. There is now emerging, we believe, a new
notion - concerned independence. To explain this notion
and why it is emerging, a survey and definition of foreign
policy options from alliance and alignment to non-
alignment is necessary. The starting point is the
emergence of sovereignty in the modern world.

Sovereignty was given a legal definition by Judge Huber
in the following terms:

> "Sovereignty in the relations between States
> signifies independence. Independence in regard
> to a portion of the globe is the right to exercise
> therein, to the exclusion of any other State,
> the functions of a State."

However, sovereignty is not purely a legal term: it
has practical components. No state enjoys the untramelled
exercise of sovereignty either in its internal or external
affairs. It is a matter of degree: the degree to which
the government's writ runs; the degree of allegiance
of the people; the degree of 'we-feeling'; the degree
to which common values are present, policies can be defined
and action taken; the degree to which the environment
can be affected. In short, sovereignty implies some
degree of external autonomy and internal order in a
territorial unit which enables political activity to
take place in both domains with a substantial degree
of independence. Sovereignty thus signifies independence,
but not necessarily self-containment and isolation.
It is independence in a world in which there is much
to be gained from interdependence but, also, one in
which independence and sovereignty can be undermined
by the coercive activity of others. Thus, those who

40

exercise soverign independence have frequently been concerned with security both internally and externally. Indeed, they have often justified their claim to authority in terms of the needs of security: the rights and duties of individuals, groups and authorities have frequently been defined in terms of security – the need to preserve sovereign independence, not in the sense of complete isolation or self-sufficiency, but in the sense of participation in world affairs on terms acceptable to the participant.

SECURITY

Security and independence are the goals of sovereignty. Yet absolute security can never be achieved and its quest has often been sought by means of alignment, and, thereby, by a curtailment of independence. Absolute security is a vain quest because it is never possible to create a situation in which no harm, whether real or perceived, can be done to an interest. So the practical political question is, how much 'insecurity' is acceptable?

There are two kinds of response to this question; one concentrates on possibilities and capabilities, the other on probabilities and intentions. It is possible that a seemingly respectable fellow-shopper will knife one in the back in a totally unprovoked and unpredictable attack, but it is a highly improbable occurrence. It is a risk to personal security that one is prepared to run. Political leaders are faced with an analogous problem in a much more violent environment. They are concerned with their own capabilities to defend the state if attacked. They are, consequently, also concerned with the capabilities of others to harm state interests. Yet they cannot put all their resources into striving to achieve absolute security since they have to respond to internal demands for 'butter' as well as for 'guns'. They, therefore, have to analyse and make a judgement about probabilities of attack and the intentions of possible adversaries, that is, the likelihood that capabilities which could threaten their interests will, in fact, be so used. However, they must be prudent since intentions can change overnight, while the necessary defence capabilities cannot be created so quickly.

The approach based on possibilities and capabilities, even tempered by judgements of probabilities, thus leads to the security policy of the armed camp. A security potential is built up on the prediction of the capabilities of others to harm a state's interests. The aim is to have the ability to deter or to parry the capabilities of others, based on the belief that whatever harm others can do, they might well do. It is a quest for as near an absolute security as possible. However, such a quest may not enhance security in practice. What appears to one side as a defensive armed camp frequently appears to others as a threat, especially when they, too, are concerned above all with capabilities. This gives rise to a competing armed camp and the search for allies with all the dangers of arms races, the growth of a war psychosis, the waste and the destruction of relationships. It thus increases the likelihood of the worst case being the actual case.

This is not the only possible approach to the safeguarding of sovereignty, independence and perceived vital interests. If there were mutually acceptable interdependences then there would be little threat to independence or sovereignty in a meaningful sense. If relationships internally, externally and transnationally were on a basis acceptable to all, then independence along with desired participation or interdependence, would be safeguarded. If any state were to try to impose undesired interdependence then it would find that the interdependent ties that it valued would be cut in retaliation. The fact of association, provided that it is on a mutually acceptable basis, creates security. The interdependent nature of that association is a hard-headed and self-interested guarantee of that security. Security by association is a policy which seeks to diminish any intention to threaten security – a sort of positive security. Alas, it, too, is not a guarantee of absolute security.

ALLIANCE

Foreign policy options, in practice, reflect elements of these two very different or opposing conceptions of security. The quest for sovereignty, independence and security is common; but the means to these ends are very different. Below, the various options are analysed by moving from the pursuit of security by means of an armed camp to security through association. Few sovereign and independent units have ever had full confidence in their ability to establish their own 'armed camp' entirely by their own resources. They have, therefore, sought safety in numbers by aligning themselves with like-minded states. An alignment is a general disposition in political and security affairs to co-operate with another Power or Powers in order to deter or prevail in the face of a possible threat. If the resulting relationship has a substantial military component then it becomes a formal alliance.

In general terms an alliance describes an understanding between two or more parties (they need not be governments) to act in concert to promote specified interests which are usually held in common and which are opposed by third parties. It is the element of potential or actual opposition by third parties, together with the willingness to coerce third parties, that is at the heart of an alliance.

In making an alliance a state seeks to enhance its position in a system of power politics and usually to manipulate the balance of power in its favour. It is seeking either to preserve or to overthrow the status quo depending upon its political values and the extent to which the status quo promotes or negates them. An alliance increases the resources at a state's command to defend its interests in a system of power politics since it is then buttressed to some degree by promises of help from its allies. However, it is also burdened by a quid pro quo - something that it must offer its allies in return. It is difficult to conceive of an alliance which does not involve some reciprocal obligations. If there were no reciprocity whatsoever then the situation would be one of an unilateral and possibly unsolicited guarantee by one party or another, whether it liked it or not. Alliances assume some common interests or goals. In practice these may be remarkably limited, where one party seeks an ally for its own particular purposes, for example, its global strategy, while its partner has very different purposes in mind in entering into the agreement, for example, its internal security. Whatever the motives, alliances in practice tend to draw lines between spheres of influence and thus to make for a clear-cut alignment of forces in a coercive situation.

COLLECTIVE SECURITY

Alliances are a technique in manipulating the balance of power. However, the balance of power is not always a successful means of managing a system of power politics. The cataclysmic example of the failure of the balance

of power to maintain stability in the international
system in 1914 gave rise to a new concept – collective
security – embodied in the Covenant of the League of
Nations. The realisation had grown that, while a balance
of power might be able to maintain an equilibrium and,
thus, a state of non-war, when the degree of instability
in the system was relatively limited, it could not handle
fundamental change in power relations in a satisfactory
manner. Nationalist movements promoted by adverse internal
conditions, revolutions and altered political systems,
uneven industrialisation and technological advances
are amongst the types of change that alter power balances
fundamentally and rapidly such that few balance of power
systems can cope.

A system of collective security is based on the notion
of a consensus among its participants, in contrast to
the balance of power system with its competing alliances
that reflect dissensus. An alliance is directed against
third parties whereas collective security is an arrangement between parties. The arrangement emanates from
a consensus about how political relations shall be
conducted. The assumption is that such relations are
normally co-operative. Disputes, however, can arise.
While peaceful change is the norm, institutional procedures
are established to facilitate the handling of disputes.
Again the assumption is that these procedures for peaceful
change and for the management of disputes are fully and
freely acceptable to all the parties. Thus, when a
contracting party does not abide by the rules for peaceful
change and the handling of disputes, collective sanctions
will be applied against it. When the basic arrangement
between the parties reflects a consensus, the need to
apply collective sanctions is a rare occurrence. When,
as was the case with the League of Nations, there is,
in effect, no original consensus involving the vanquished
(Germany) and the outcast (the Soviet Union) and even
some of the victors are disgruntled (Italy and Japan),
collective security quickly degenerates into a system
of power politics with competing alliances. Thus,
collective security is, in theory at least, in sharp
contrast to alliance systems and the balance of power.
It is not a threat system. It is an agreement to abide
by a set of rules of behaviour. With legitimised methods
of peaceful change, the need for sanctions should be
rare. However, it only has these attributes when it
is based upon a continuing consensus. It faces, therefore,
the same problem of handling fundamental change as the
balance of power and has fared no better.

NEUTRALITY

Collective security has not been the only escape mechanism from the dangerous confrontations of alliance politics. Some states have chosen neutrality. <u>Neutrality</u> is a legal status embodying rights and duties for third parties <u>vis-à-vis</u> belligerents. Thus it can only come into operation when a war has been declared or a state of hostilities is deemed to be in existence. In the logic of international law it is impossible to be neutral in times of peace. Behaviour, however, does not always conform to the exigencies of international law. Some states have been permanently neutralised, others have declared themselves to be neutral permanently and some have had wide recognition of their self-proclamation.

A recognised condition of neutrality has a formal element of unlimited duration. The permanent nature of the neutrality involves additional rights and duties between the neutralised state, the guarantors of its neutrality (usually the great Powers) and the other actors in the system. These involve not only an expressed willingness and the ability always to be neutral in time of war, but the taking of such action in time of peace as may be deemed necessary both by the neutral and by the system to give credibility to the undertaking to be neutral in time of war. This assumes that a neutral state cannot participate in peacetime alliances, that it will defend its neutrality diplomatically, economically and, if need be, militarily. Moreover, it will strive to preserve that element of national unit necessary to remove any likelihood of external intervention in its domestic affairs prejudicial to its external neutrality. In foreign policy the neutralised state does not assume any obligations likely to compromise its neutralised status.

The main difference between a state which has had its neutrality imposed by others and a self-proclaimed neutralised state is that the former has no choice in the matter. However, in practice this is of little consequence since the historic examples of imposed neutralisation, at least in Europe, have all been with the consent of the government and people of the neutralised state. A further major difference remains in that a neutralised state has a special relationship with its guarantors. It may receive a collective guarantee of its neutrality by the major Powers of the system or a guarantee from an individual country or both. In this relationship the guarantors agree not only to respect the neutrality of the state concerned but also to ensure that others do as well. For its part the neutral state's government and people undertake to follow the dictates of neutrality both in the letter and in the spirit. On the other hand, a self-proclaimed neutral may seek to persuade the great Powers of the day of its permanent neutrality and, thereby, to elicit some acknowledgement and, indeed, guarantee of its status. It nevertheless has the option of changing its status by its own volition without generally giving rise to serious consequences for the political system as a whole.

However, permanent neutrality is not always respected nor is indirect violation of neutrality a problem with which it is easy to deal. Violations of neutrality of recognised neutrals usually occur in two circumstances. Since such neutrals are often in the eye of a system of power politics and are, therefore, valuable prizes, violations occur when the balance of power that gave rise to their original recognition has changed. The second form of violation occurs when the internal balance is disturbed. Thus it is not enough that there should be initial internal and international consensus for neutralisation: that consensus must also be maintained. All the major actors – internal and external – must, therefore, see it to be in their continued interest to maintain, and, if necessary, to defend the status of the neutral. The problem is again one of change for which power balances are, in the long run, ineffective and potentially catastrophic.

A variant of neutrality as an escape from the alliance systems of power politics is isolation, which is not a policy open to many states in the contemporary world. Perhaps the classic exposition of this position was that of George Washington, the first President of the USA, in his Farewell Address:

> "The great rule of conduct for us in regard to foreign nations is, in extending our commercial relations to have with them as little <u>political</u> connection as possible ......
>
> Europe has a set of primary interests which to us have none or a very remote relation. Hence she must be engaged in frequent controversies,

the causes of which are essentially foreign to
our concerns. Hence, therefore it must be unwise
in us to implicate ourselves by artifical ties
in the ordinary vicissitudes of her politics
or the ordinary combinations and collisions of
her friendships or enmities ......

Why forego the advantages of so peculiar a
situation? Why quit our own to stand upon
foreign ground? Why, by interweaving our destiny
with that of any part of Europe, entangle our
peace and prosperity in the toils of European
Ambition, Rivalship, Interest, Humor, or Caprice?"

- a sentiment that Europeans might now share in respect
of the super Powers. However, this is an understandable
reaction for a newly independent state. Its contemporary
expression in an interdependent world is non-alignment
- a policy which has been chosen by a majority of the
newly independent countries.

NON-ALIGNMENT

These states have decided that to join alliances in the
contemporary world is more detrimental to their own and
the community interest than to adopt a non-aligned stance.
Non-aligned states are not passive or neutral; they
are in favour of an active interest and concern in world
politics at all levels. Since they are in a loose
consultative association of a non-binding character,
they do not, and do not wish, to form a bloc. Indeed,
they seek to overcome the dangerous consequences of bloc
politics. They want, in a non-discriminatory manner,
to make an independent judgement on the issues of the
day and to participate in their management. Moreover,
they pursue an independent approach to the parties based
on the issues in dispute, even if on a specific question
they come down on a particular side. Thus, there is
no unified non-aligned position, since different non-
aligned countries will, through the exercise of their
independent judgement, come to different conclusions.
Nevertheless, by pursuing their individual interests
in an awareness of a world community interest and an
acknowledgement of fellow feeling for others, they do
contrive to arrive at a consensus.

In order to be non-aligned a state must not be dependent
in an exclusive or coerced manner in any major dimension

of its activities - political, economic, social, military, cultural - either internally or externally. Non-aligned states are neither isolationist nor autarkic, they are interdependent. Their interdependence has certain important characteristics: it is not exclusive in the sense of a dependence on one other state or group of states. Relationships are balanced between partners and between dimensions so that a dominant flow in one direction in, say, cultural ties, will be compensated for in, say, the economic domain both in terms of partner and direction of flow. However, it is difficult to be a non-aligned state when there are serious internal disharmonies, since disaffected groups turn to external sources for succour. This can lead to an association of internal forces with external states, thus creating alliance linkages across the state's boundaries.

A non-aligned stance can be in relation to all external ties in all dimensions or limited to a specific set of transactions. A state can avoid permanent ties with any actor in relation to any situation. It can approach issues in a spirit of independent judgement and can, in so doing, pursue its own interest with a conscious awareness of the interests of others and of the community at large. Alternatively, it can act in a non-aligned manner towards a particular set of relationships, but not necessarily universally. Thus India has acted largely in a non-aligned manner in the Cold War, but in an aligned manner in the Sino-Soviet dispute. The same may be said of the non-aligned movement as a whole vis-à-vis the East-West and North-South issues. Non-alignment leads to some states playing a supportive third party role in regard to the parties in systems of power politics. They endeavour to move such systems towards the resolution of conflicts and the establishment of more legitimised relationships.

Thus non-alignment is conceived as a policy of independence and independent judgement on world issues. Furthermore - and it is this which is important to the world society - it is a policy of states that are not in a position to participate in the power politics system and a policy, therefore, which seeks national security through peaceful relations. Inevitably, the independent judgement exercised must, if the policy is to succeed, take into consideration elements of law, justice, development and human welfare in addition to short term security.

Non-alignment, however, has fallen short of an active and institutionalised third party role in relation to the major conflicts that threaten world peace. Perhaps this is because it is a policy adopted by small and relatively weak states. Perhaps it is also because many of these states are plagued with internal economic and political instability. While the _policy_ retains its political vitality and it has a powerful logic, the non-aligned _movement_ in its contemporary guise has lost its way. India, through Nehru (who was very wary of the movement) was the first, consciously, to follow the policy, has now through its Chairmanship of the movement taken on the task of putting the movement back on the rails by taking it back to the first principles of the policy.

CONCERNED INDEPENDENCE

Without detracting from the many endeavours neutral and non-aligned states have made separately and together at the UN and in other ways to promote a more just and peaceful international system, we are introducing the notion of _Concerned Independence_ to signify a more influential and positive role in world affairs. This is the role we advocate for Britain.

Most dictionaries provide an adequate basis for an understanding of the term. Independence or the state of being independent can mean: not subject to control by others; self-governing; not affiliated with a larger controlling unit; not requiring or relying upon somebody else; not looking to others for one's opinions or for the guidance of one's conduct; not bound by or committed definitively to a political party; refusing to accept assistance or to be under obligation to others; showing a desire for freedom and absence of constraint. However, in modern times, it is less likely that the word would have an absolute meaning and that a state either would be or would not be wholly independent. It is more a question of the degree to which it is independent, from whom and the purpose for which such independence is sought.

To this must be added the notion of concern. Concern does not imply self-abnegation, but merely that self-interests are seen in the context of community interest. It is an acknowledgement that in the long run it is self-defeating to pursue self-interests in a self-centred fashion when they are contrary to community interest.

There is a practical reason for this. Everyone is dependent to some degree on community services and few can get away with being a 'free rider' without there being retaliation on the part of the community or a collapse of community services. Concern, therefore, connotes an acknowledgement of community interest and a willingness to contribute to it. However, it is more than that. It is, also, an open acknowledgement of others: it implies a genuine endeavour to adjust policies where they are in conflict with others, a refusal to revert to coercion and power politics automatically and immediately in order to settle disputes, an attempt to be supportive of <u>all</u> the parties in disputes that involve others. It is an approach that defines conflict as a mutual problem to be resolved in a manner which is satisfactory to all parties rather than to seek to 'win' or to impose a 'compromise'. Concerned independence, then, is more than the sovereignty and independence associated with the 'security' of the armed camp described in this Chapter. Sovereignty, independence and security remain important, but they must be sought in an interdependent world. Ultimately, security can be found only in mutually acceptable relationships – security by association.

It cannot be gainsayed that the contemporary world is economically, politically, militarily and even culturally and socially interdependent. Why, then, independence? Independence does not necessarily connote isolation or autarky: it is an attitude of mind and a guide for policies which seek to maximise openness and diversity. It implies choosing a policy on the basis of merits of the case seen in the light of values such as participation, self-interest and community interests couched in a supportive framework. In no sense is it a soft option, but it may be a rewarding role both for the society adopting it and the wider community. It strives for the ideal of an active policy which supports peace and security, not through confrontation and the manipulation of threat systems, but through a problem solving approach to differences. The achievement of peace and security is sought through the encouragement and development of cross-cutting and transnational ties between states and the development of shared community goals to create a 'working peace system' which maximises the benefits of both independence and interdependence without the dangers of the 'separate peace systems' of rival armed camps.

Concerned independence differs fundamentally from neutrality or a passive foreign policy. It connotes a very active participation in world relationships and a vigorous foreign policy. It implies the exercise of the right to independent participation in world events. It often requires that those pursuing a policy of concerned independence be able to demonstrate their own domestic independence. This does not mean that an independent policy cannot be followed by a society with many outside links. It is, however, an interdependent society that is also an open society in the sense that it is not linked exclusively to one bloc, group or country in any major area and all its ties are mutually acceptable in content and in form. It should also be borne in mind that independence is a prime contemporary value: it is the path to participation and it enhances a sense of identity. In other words, an independent country is one that has non-exclusive and non-coercive political, economic, security and cultural roles.

For an independent country following a policy of concerned independence in the contemporary world, the East-West and the North-South issues are crucial. It is concerned independence in these two dimensions that forms the basis of a new stance in world affairs. The independence is not only for the pursuit of purely national interests, but also to enhance community interests embracing all parties in the context of these issues. There has to be a strong element of self-reliance, yet there has to be a studied openness to a variety of transaction systems. The role of an independent and concerned state in a power politics relationship is to play a supportive third party role in a non-directive, non-judgemental and problem solving manner. The principal contemporary conflicts include the East-West and North-South confrontations. By attempting to ameliorate the conflicts in these two dimensions an independent state would not only be providing for its own security, but also for that of others. Insofar as the East-West conflict is concerned détente in the 1960s and 1970s has shown that amelioration of the East-West dispute is possible and, indeed, that the Helsinki framework is one that can be made much of in a positive way. The Final Act is a promissory note rather than a contract by which the parties can be sued. It provides an opportunity to begin in those areas where whole-hearted co-operation is possible and then to seek to improve conditions in other areas. If the 'best' is unattainable the 'better' is something to be going on with and should not be scorned.

In the North-South dimension the Brandt report has set
out a possible way forward and one that is in the interests
of both North and South. But it requires leadership
and a massive programme of education in the necessity
for unpalatable policies in the short term for both the
North and the South in order to gain long term advantages.

An independent policy means moving away from exclusive
ties. It does not necessarily mean cutting ties, but
rather that relationships should be open and more diverse.
Indeed, the extent to which this diversity grows may
in some way be correlated with the degree of security
experienced, because if an independent country with
valued and valuable ties with many different actors
were ever threatened then all those actors would be involved.
In this sense security comes from a policy of concerned
independence which includes the building-up of a vast
range of acceptable and freely accepted relationships.

The past is not inevitably the future and the contemporary
alliance systems are not immutable. They are a palliative
against a worse world. At some point these alliance
systems will cease - perhaps as a result of a holocaust,
perhaps because of the growth of more acceptable East-
West relations. An independent and concerned state
can make a 'working peace system' more, not less likely.
It can do this by adopting a third party role and
attempting to promote a problem solving approach, which
seeks to maximise the totality of values of all parties
in conflict, instead of power bargaining and the half-
way house of compromise which somehow tries to share
dissatisfactions by 'splitting the difference'. Concerned
independence is thus a security policy for the contemporary
world since it is based on the premise that security
is indivisible - no group is fully secure while others
feel insecure. It suggests that independence is a highly
prized contemporary norm, but that it is not incompatible
with interdepenence (the benefits of which are potentially
great) when linkages are non-exclusive and non-coercive.
Finally, it implies concern; concern not just with
self-interests, but also with the interests of others
and 'the community at large because without such joint
concerns the values and benefits of independence and
interdependence are threatened. It is thus a policy
of enlightened self-interest in a dangerous and deterio-
rating world.

5 Neutralism: the European experience

NEUTRALITY: A LEGAL CONCEPT

Neutrality, one of the foreign policy options described in Chapter Four, has existed throughout the history of the European state system. Sometimes it has been adopted in a determination to pursue an independent foreign policy. In other cases it has been imposed upon states in the interests of greater Powers, rather than in those of the neutral itself.

Britain has not had the experience of neutrality in any form in its long history of European relations. It is still a strange notion to most Britons. Its history in Western Europe may have something to contribute to British policy making in the contemporary world.

Until the Second World War neutrality was essentially a passive policy, an opting out of the existing balance of power system. But in the last 35 years active neutralism has often been a dynamic foreign policy aimed at improving the international atmosphere while abstaining from the East-West confrontation which has dominated the international system. This Chapter explores the changes which have taken place in the concept of neutrality and examines what neutrality means to six European states: Switzerland, Sweden, Austria, Finland, Yugoslavia and Ireland.

Neutrality, in the sense of non-participation in wars between other states, has existed for as long as war has existed. It has often been in the interests of belligerents to prevent an increase in the number of their enemies. It has usually been in the interest of some states to remain uninvolved in war. The concept of neutral rights and duties arose from these common interests. When international relations assumed a legalistic character in the seventeenth and eighteenth centuries, neutrality was given legal status: in law and in practice it was recognized that it was the duty of neutrals to remain impartial and the duty of belligerents to respect the territorial integrity of neutrals.

By the nineteenth century neutralisation, that is an enforced or guaranteed status of neutrality, was seen as a means of preserving the balance of power. In the aftermath of the Napoleonic wars Switzerland reverted to its previous neutrality. After this status was guaranteed by the European great Powers at the Congress of Vienna in 1815, permanent neutrality became part of the law of nations for the first time. Belgian neutrality was guaranteed in 1839 and the neutrality of Luxembourg in 1867. Meanwhile, the United States of America had withdrawn from the European balance of power with Washington's farewell address, a policy of neutrality based on political isolation at least as far as Europe was concerned.

The legal basis of neutrality and the extent to which it was seen to apply only to times of war, is emphasised by the kinds of provisions laid down in the Hague Conventions of 1907, which codified the rights and duties of neutrals and those of belligerents. Neutrals were to use force to prevent violations of their neutrality, they could allow passage to the sick and wounded of a belligerent, but not to troops. They were to observe strict impartiality towards belligerents. Belligerents could punish any breach of neutrality and had, also, to refrain from using neutral territory in any way. In the Hague Conventions a distinction is made between the neutrality of the state and the neutrality of its nationals. The neutrality of the state does not require impartial behaviour from its citizens. This double standard is a product of the laissez-faire society which preceded the First World War. In that international society the profit motive was sacrosanct and any encroachment by the state was considered improper. The role of the state was confined to politics and politics was narrowly defined.

Although both the nature of the state and the nature of war have changed, the Hague conventions and other conventions, which exist as part of customary law, continue to govern the mutual wartime behaviour between neutrals and belligerents. The legal concept of neutrality is strikingly silent about the peacetime behaviour of neutrals, since neutrality in the legal sense pre-supposes war. However, as war has become less localised and as the means of waging war have increased, so a self-declared policy of neutrality or even guaranteed neutralisation has become increasingly difficult to sustain. Only small states distant from the theatre of war have maintained their neutrality easily in the twentieth century and then only if belligerents have preferred those states to be neutral. Thus, after the outbreak of the First World War, Switzerland and Sweden remained neutral, while Luxembourg was occupied by Germany. When Germany attacked Belgium, France and Britain went to war.

After the First World War, it seemed that a policy of neutrality was redundant. War had been outlawed and the collective security system of the League of Nations would deter potential aggressors from waging war. Since strict neutrality was inconsistent with membership of the League, which obliged members to apply sanctions against aggressor states, neutral policies were condemned. It was only in the late 'thirties that it became clear that the system of collective security had broken down irrevocably. Many of the smaller European states like Denmark, Holland, Norway, Belgium, Ireland and Finland reverted to neutrality. The fate of these countries in the Second World War re-emphasised the lessons of the Great War: in any widespread and prolonged war, the rights of neutrals will be little regarded.

In the struggle to contain Hitler, those who were against appeasement saw neutrality as insipid, humiliating and immoral. In the post war world, when the struggle shifted to the capitalist-communist divide, neutralism was considered by both bloc leaders to be the appeasement of the other. Only the traditional neutrals like Switzerland and Sweden were exempt, by the West, from these charges. States which had made great sacrifices to win the war held the principles of neutralisation, neutrality and neutralism in low esteem. A commitment to fight against dictatorship was regarded as a higher value than a commitment to peace. One of the conditions of admission to the founding conference of the United Nations in 1945 was that states declare war on Germany and its allies in order to demonstrate their desire for peace. By the time the conference met the world was beginning to be polarised into Western and Soviet blocs. In the view of each side, states which were not unambiguously for them were by definition against them. In any case the United Nations was to provide a new collective security system which would render neutrality irrelevant.

The United Nations Charter does not recognise the status of neutrality as a matter of right. Although it is more flexible than the League Covenant in its demands upon member states for sanctions against an aggressor, there are serious problems regarding the compatibility of membership of the United Nations with a status of permanent neutrality. In 1945 Switzerland decided against UN membership. In contrast Austria was admitted to the United Nations after it had adopted a constitutional law asserting perpetual neutrality. Other European neutrals like Sweden, Ireland and Finland, are members of the United Nations. This indicates that there are differences in the way in which neutralism is interpreted. There are also differences in the way in which neutralism is practised by the six European neutrals. Even more significantly, attitudes towards neutrals have changed substantially. Neutralism now often evokes respect and admiration, perhaps even a sneaking desire to emulate. In part this reflects a growing awareness that the alliance systems of East and West have contributed little to international security and even less to the acute problems of North-South relations. It is also caused by the changing nature of neutralism itself. As the legal status of neutrality has lost significance and the underlying political concepts have become more important, so the way in which the European neutrals participate in the international system has changed. Switzerland, Sweden, Austria, Finland, Ireland and Yugoslavia have become neutral for different reasons, they define their neutrality variously and they do not practise identical policies. Nevertheless, they have in common an authoritative voice and a valuable role in international affairs as the recent conclusion of the Madrid Security Conference attests.

SWITZERLAND AND NEUTRALITY

The Swiss interpretation of neutrality was restated officially in 1954. It is an essentially conservative concept, although it does not denote an inert foreign policy. As a permanent neutral, Switzerland is committed to a policy of neutrality both in wartime and in peacetime. This obviously means that Switzerland must abstain from starting war and must defend its neutrality. It must also avoid policies and actions which might involve it in future hostilities. For this reason Switzerland must not adhere to any treaty involving a political commitment with other states. It cannot participate in an economic union which might jeopardise its political independence. Similarly, Switzerland will not join the collective security arrangements of the United Nations, although it participates in those international conferences and organisations which are of a predominantly economic, cultural or technical nature. Switzerland can offer good offices or mediation during conflicts and crises.

In practice this means that Switzerland is a member of the European Free Trade Area; but it has not joined the European Communities. Although it does not belong to the United Nations, it has participated in many of its activities, including serving on the Supervisory Commission on Korea and co-operating in peace-keeping operations. It belongs to the United Nations Specialised Agencies like UNESCO, the Food and Agricultural Organisation, the World Meteorological Organisation and the International Atomic Energy Agency. Switzerland is often used as the location for international conferences and it is the headquarters for a large number of international organisations, governmental and non-governmental. The International Committee of the Red Cross, the organisation which the Swiss see as the best expression of the beneficial and humanitarian nature of their neutrality, has its headquarters in Geneva and recruits its directing personnel from Swiss citizens.

The role of Switzerland as a centre of international finance and commerce and as the headquarters of a wide variety of international organisations has reinforced its neutrality: a potential aggressor would have to deal with the enmity which the loss of Swiss financial and commercial services would arouse in countries which depend upon these services. However, the Swiss do not rely on the indispensability of these functions to defend their neutrality. During the two world wars Swiss military readiness was a significant factor in deterring violation of its neutrality. Although Switzerland had a relatively small army, it was well enough organised to ensure that no belligerent could attack Switzerland without withdrawing forces from other theatres of war. Moreover, the Swiss could blow up the tunnels under the Alps to prevent any army crossing Switzerland. Although its geographic location means that Switzerland could not escape the consequences of a nuclear war, Switzerland continues to rely on conventional defence, with a conscript army and a great deal of attention given to civil defence. While both East and West seem to agree that Swiss sympathies are with the West, this has scarcely tainted Swiss neutrality in the eyes of the Soviet Union. Nor has it shaken Swiss belief in the unique nature of Swiss neutrality.

SWEDEN

Sweden, too, has a venerable tradition of neutrality, dating from 1815. Sweden is also a neutral which tilts towards the West without this affecting its credibility. The Swedish concept of neutrality is rather more pragmatic than that of the Swiss. Sweden declared itself neutral when the First World War began and maintained its neutrality in part because of its favourable geographic position. At the end of the war it was one of the thirteen neutral states to become original members of the League of Nations. It seemed to have no difficulty in reconciling the demands of collective security with neutrality. When collective security broke down in January 1938, Sweden was the first of the neutrals to announce that it had lost confidence in the League and was rearming. During the Second World War Sweden combined neutrality with an active policy of aid to the other Scandinavian countries, while supplying war materials to both sides. It also provided humanitarian and diplomatic services. Sweden does not see membership of the United Nations as being inconsistent with neutrality: it has been a member since 1946. It is also a member of the European Free Trade Area and of the Nordic Council.

Like the Swiss, the Swedes are conscious that a neutrality which can be seen to be of international benefit is more likely to be respected than a policy of neutral isolation. So Sweden has sent medical aid to Korea, taken part in

the United Nations Supervisory Commission on Korea and
it has taken an active part in United Nations disarmament
conferences. It has also contributed military contingents
to UN forces.

Swedish neutrality is defended by a conscript army,
an airforce and a navy, renowned for their training,
their skill and their modern military techniques. Sweden,
like Switzerland, pays much attention to civil defence.
Given its strategic position, semi-encircled by the USSR
and two NATO members, Sweden would not be able to defend
its neutrality in any future war in northern Europe.
Nonetheless, neutrality, without disengagement from world
affairs, continues to be the foreign policy advocated
by the important political parties in Sweden.

AUSTRIA

While the Swedes have chosen neutrality and the Swiss
have made it a vocation, the Austrians have had neutrality
thrust upon them. It was the price Austria paid for
independence and sovereignty after ten years of post
war four-power occupation. It was the product of astute
diplomacy on the part of Austrian politicians and of
a reassessment of Soviet strategic and diplomatic concerns
after the death of Stalin. In the bitterness which
immediately beset the alliance once the war was over,
a peace treaty with Germany became the condition for
Austrian independence in Soviet foreign policy. Since
the erstwhile allies could not reach agreement on Germany,
Austria continued to be occupied. On the new map of Europe,
Austria had replaced Switzerland as the crossroads of
Europe, located on the dividing line between two antagonistic alliance systems. Removing Austria from
contention between the two blocs was the only way in
which a basis could be found for an agreement that would
return Austrian statehood without disturbing the existing
balance of power in Central Europe. Austrian neutrality
was negotiated bilaterally by the Austrian and Soviet
governments, as a result of which the Austrian State
Treaty was signed in May 1955. In October 1955 the Austrian
parliament enacted a Constitutional Federal Statute
declaring permanent neutrality. Austria would not join
any military alliance, it would ban foreign military
bases and it would not accept any political or economic
obligations which could impair its neutrality. The
four occupying Powers and other states with which Austria
had diplomatic relations recognised Austrian neutrality

formally, but without any guarantees to defend it.

It was the Soviet intention, and it is specifically mentioned in formal Austrian declarations, that Austrian neutralism should be based on the Swiss model. In fact, it resembles a combination of Swedish and Swiss neutrality. Austria was admitted to membership of the United Nations in December 1955 without any reservation, though some international lawyers contend that its permanent neutrality and membership of the United Nations cannot be juridically reconciled. Austria is a member of the Council of Europe and of the European Free Trade Area. Soviet objections have prevented it seeking membership of the European Communities.

Apart from the predominant obligation to remain neutral in the rivalry between the Soviet and Western blocs, Austria considers itself free to participate in any international organisation so long as it does not have a military character. The diplomatic skill of Austrian politicians is demonstrated by the way in which Austria manages to keep on good terms with both super Powers, even though it openly evinces its affinities with the West and provides temporary shelter for emigrées from Eastern Europe. It also provides the location for international organisations of various political inclinations and is often the stage for international negotiations and conferences.

Under the terms of the Austrian State Treaty, Austria may not possess nuclear weapons; but there is no limit to the size of the Austrian army. Given its strategic position, there can be no Austrian army large enough to defend Austrian neutrality in the case of war in Europe. In fact its armed forces are small.

FINLAND

Three other European states, Finland, Yugoslavia and Ireland, follow a self-declared policy of neutrality. Irish membership of the European Communities diminishes the credibility of Irish neutrality in the eyes of Soviet politicians. Finnish dependence on Soviet goodwill annuls Finnish neutrality in Western perception. Both East and West sometimes distrust Yugoslavia's non-alignment. Nonetheless, all three states follow neutral policies which allow them to offer credible good services in the international arena.

Like Austria, Finland owes its neutral status to Soviet security concerns. In 1939 a declared policy of neutrality had proved impotent in the face of Soviet determination to move its vulnerable border with Finland further away from Leningrad. After initial Finnish victories, the Winter War of 1939-40 ended with Finland ceding more territory to the Soviet Union than had originally been demanded. When Germany invaded the Soviet Union in June 1941, Finland too declared war on the Soviet Union, though with no clear commitment to Germany. Finland signed a cease-fire with the Soviet Union in September 1944. The Finnish army expelled German soldiers from Finland without waiting for Soviet aid, so that when the war ended there was no Soviet army of occupation in Finland. However, it had become clear to Finnish citizens and their leaders that the price of a Western-type democracy and of even limited sovereignty was a perpetual assurance to Soviet leaders that their security needs would be satisfied.

When Stalin demanded that Finland sign a Mutual Assistance Treaty in 1948, skilful Finnish politicians managed to negotiate a more limited treaty than those signed by other statesmen of Eastern Europe. While Finland guaranteed that any attack on the Soviet Union through Finland would be resisted, consultation between the two countries on military questions would take place only if a threat of aggression existed. There would be no Soviet military aid without a Finnish request for such aid. Moreover, the preamble to the treaty makes explicit 'Finland's desire to remain outside the conflicting interests of the great Powers'. Even before international recognition of Finland's neutral policy, Finnish claims to neutrality were based on that phrase and Finnish foreign policy has been dominated by that theme, combined with the need to assuage Soviet sensibilities. Reassuring the Soviet Union requires the designing of Finnish domestic and foreign policies in ways which do not exacerbate Soviet security fears. It is this situation which is called Finlandisation and it is feared by some in the West as a potential model for Soviet domination of Western Europe.

By 1956 Soviet leaders had begun referring to Finland as a neutral state. Western leaders followed suit in the early 'sixties, despite the fact that the Soviet-Finnish Mutual Assistance Treaty had been extended for a further twenty years. By this time Finland had been admitted to the United Nations. In 1955 it had also joined the Nordic Council, a consultative organ linking

Norway, Sweden, Denmark, Iceland and Finland which deals with many common problems but excludes any defence matters. Nordic co-operation and interdependence in areas of low politics have grown over the years, in spite of the fact that, of the states involved, two are neutral and three belong to the North Atlantic Treaty Organisation.

Finnish politicians compare Finland's role in the international system to that of a physician or describe it as 'bridge-building'. At first the medical role was exercised by Finnish participation in United Nations peace making and peace keeping operations. Later a more ambitious Finnish foreign policy aimed to involve the country in a series of multilateral relationships such that its neutral status would not be jeopardized. Thus Finland did not join the European Free Trade Area immediately, but, after long negotiations with the Soviet Union, a new organisation, FINEFTA, was created to handle Finnish membership without threatening Soviet Union trade advantages in Finland. Similarly, a free trade agreement was signed with the European Economic Community in 1972, followed by an agreement on co-operation with Comecon in 1973.

Finnish active neutrality envisages a Europe bound together by a series of cross-cutting relationships, overlapping countries with different social and political systems and belonging to different military blocs. Their multilateral contacts, neutral status and the special relationship with the Soviet Union, uniquely qualify the Finns to act as middlemen and mediators of ideas in international negotiations. A great deal of Finnish diplomatic activity preceded the European Conference on Security and Co-operation, hosted by Finland, and Finland was proud to provide facilities for the super Power strategic arms limitations talks.

Finnish neutrality relies on the ability of Finnish politicians to reduce the possibility of super Power conflict and, failing that, to remove Finland as much as possible from areas of possible tension. Finland does not have a military capability which could defend its neutrality. The possession of such a capability could itself endanger Finnish neutrality, since it might encourage the Soviet Union to insist that Finland joins the Warsaw Treaty Organisation. Though the Soviet Union does not officially recognize the concept of a 'Northern Balance', the minimal Finnish commitment to the treaty with the Soviet Union is acceptable because Sweden is neutral, while Norway and Denmark, though members of NATO, do not have NATO bases, nor do they permit the stationing of nuclear weapons on their territory.

YUGOSLAVIA

Although the term non-alignment tends to be associated with the foreign policy of southern Third World states, the fifth European neutral, Yugoslavia, was one of the founders of the movement. To a certain extent the Soviet Union is also responsible for Yugoslav non-alignment, since it was when Yugoslavia was expelled from the Soviet bloc in 1948 that it became necessary to develop a new international doctrine to legitimize non-members of the major blocs. Non-alignment was launched as a concept and a policy in the 'forties and 'fifties and it became a movement in the 'sixties. It has become important both in East-West and in North-South relations. However, for Yugoslavia, geographically, economically, politically and ideologically between West and East, non-alignment remains essential in the context of super Power relations, East-West antagonism and co-operation and, perhaps even more, in the context of conflict within the Soviet bloc.

Stalin's expulsion of Yugoslavia from Cominform was followed by economic sanctions which necessitated new trade links with the West if Yugoslavia was to survive. By the time Stalin's successors had moderated their anti-Yugoslav policy, Yugoslavia had discovered the importance of the United Nations for small, weak nations. Contact and interaction with the newly-independent nations in the United Nations led Yugoslavia to seek an association that was ideologically congenial, politically feasible and strategically secure. Tito had dropped his previous territorial demands on neighbouring states and a period of peaceful coexistence in the Balkans followed. Active coexistence became the theme of Yugslav foreign policy and non-alignment was seen as an implicit prerequisite and inevitable consequence of active coexistence.

For Yugoslav leaders, non-alignment did not denote a reluctance to take sides in times of crisis, nor did it require limiting political activity to the United Nations or the non-aligned movement, though full use was made of these. Tito pursued a vigorous diplomacy in an attempt to prevent crises turning into armed conflicts, particularly within the Soviet bloc. When five countries of the Warsaw Treaty Organisation intervened in Czechoslovakia in 1968, Tito decided to raise the cost of any attempt to intervene in Yugoslavia and to convince both blocs that they need not fear Yugoslavia siding with the other. The doctrine of the General People's Defence was introduced in 1969. Under threat of aggression, Yugoslavia intends turning itself into a nation under arms in a matter of hours and promises to resist until the 'last man'.

IRELAND

Neutrality was a psychological necessity for Ireland between the wars, a demonstration of sovereignty and, more importantly, of independence from Britain. By 1939, as for so many other small European Powers, neutrality had become a logical security policy. However, Irish wartime neutrality, interpreted by the Soviet Union as open sympathy for the Axis Powers, delayed Irish membership of the United Nations until 1955. In any case, in the immediate post war period Ireland was content to be 'the island behind the island'. Irish foreign policy was obsessed with partition and membership of NATO was rejected primarily because of a reluctance to join an alliance with Britain in addition to a distaste for the alliance systems of the Cold War.

Admission to the United Nations in 1955 caused a shift in Irish foreign policy from isolation to a more dynamic neutrality based on support for the United Nations Charter. Although Irish spokesmen declared Ireland to be independent of Cold War blocs within the United Nations, Irish sympathies were overtly on the side of preservation of Christian civilisation and supported those countries determined to resist the spread of communist power and influence. The new Irish foreign policy manifested itself in participation in United Nations peace keeping efforts and increasing activity in the field of disarmament and arms control. Within Ireland a new pride was expressed in Ireland's mediatory influence and its ability to create a more favourable international environment. Neutrality had become an article of faith, rather than a pragmatic reaction to a dangerous world situation or a refusal to be associated with Britain.

When Ireland joined the European Communities in 1973, the political consequences of membership were never openly discussed in Ireland. Unlike other European neutrals, Ireland does not seem to find membership of the Communities inconsistent with its neutral foreign policy.

NEUTRALITY - A POSITIVE POLICY

	Membership of:			Credible Defence Force	Active International Participation
	United Nations	EC	Other regional international organisations		
Austria	Yes	No	Yes	No	Yes
Finland	Yes	No	Yes	No	Yes
Ireland	Yes	Yes	Yes	No	Yes
Sweden	Yes	No	Yes	Yes	Yes
Switzer-land	No	No	Yes	Yes	Yes
Yugo-slavia	Yes	No	Yes	Yes	Yes

In each of the six European cases described, neutrality is defined and practised differently. A glance at the table above shows that all the neutrals, except Switzerland, belong to the United Nations. Only Ireland found membership of the EC consistent with neutrality, though all six belong to purely functional, non-political regional international organisations. Only Yugoslavia belongs to the non-aligned movement, though other neutrals have attended non-aligned conferences as observers. Only Sweden, Switzerland and Yugoslavia possess a substantial military capability. With the exception of Ireland, they form a link between Western and Eastern Europe.

In all six cases, the old image of neutrality as a toothless impotence proclaimed by states who have been bypassed by the turbulence of history has disappeared. Neutrality has acquired international legitimacy and respect, it can be seen to be an active and independent policy which has the potential to mitigate or to prevent conflict and war. Neutral states can create a buffer between antagonistic alliances, so benefitting international security. In addition, they can provide special diplomatic, financial, peace keeping and problem solving services to the international community. This is different from the traditional role of neutrals. Neutrality no longer implies opting out of responsibility and giving up an honoured place in the international corridors of power. The European neutrals may not be powerful in the conventional sense in which the power of a state used to be measured; but they are an increasingly strong force in an interdependent world, which can survive only if co-operation replaces confrontation in the essential international attempts to resolve problems which become ever more intractable.

The European experience suggests that neutrality depends in part upon domestic stability and a unity of purpose which is committed to neutrality no matter which political party or coalition is in power. It depends even more heavily upon credibility, which itself requires both a domestic consensus about neutrality and a consistently independent response to external events.

Neutrality also depends upon foreign recognition and respect for neutral status. In a nuclear world there can be no question of defending neutrality by military means, so perhaps the will to defend neutrality by force of arms is no longer necessary to be credible. However, the European experience also suggests that an active, committed neutrality could help to prevent a cold war from becoming a shooting war in which neutrality needs to be defended.

As already observed, neutrality in any form is a strange notion to the people of Britain. It connotes something negative and the absence of any effective leadership or a power-balancing role. However, this long European experience shows that neutrality can take any form and can be a positive policy in relation to particular situations. One form that it is edging towards in Europe is a consistent and active third party role in relation to East-West tensions generally. This trend would be much strengthened by the adhesion of a state that has previously had a long experience as a main actor - Germany, France or Britain. Is the island, Britain, to be once again, but by quite different means, the key actor in preserving peace in Western Europe and in the international system generally?

6 The Third World experience

NON-ALIGNMENT: TRANSITION FROM COERCIVE POLITICS

We have seen that the historical evolution of the world system places non-alignment in a significant position: it signifies a transition stage between a coercive politics approach to security and the notion of security relying upon a network of mutually acceptable relationships in the international system. This stage emerged as a consequence of the changes that took place in the structure of world society after the Second World War. Decolonisation led to the creation of about a hundred new and, for the most part, relatively powerless independent states. It was inevitable that they should seek separately and in consultation with one another, non-coercive means by which to maintain their independence and security, while at the same time taking advantage of any aid they could obtain from the more powerful states. In doing so they created the concept of non-alignment.

Transition is the relevant term, for we suggest that this new notion is relevant to states that were previously powerful and which, in the new circumstances of the nuclear age and the interdependence which has accompanied it, cannot achieve security solely through alliances and the balance of power. French policy under de Gaulle and Mitterand and British policy under Macmillan have taken some steps in this direction. However, the newly-independent countries adopted the policy whole-heartedly to the extent of becoming a thorn in the side of both protagonists in the Cold War and were condemned by both at one stage or another. Their policies have been inconsistent and ambiguous. Yet they have made an important contribution to world society by the creation of the notion that independence and non-alignment of some kind, could be the norm in world affairs. For large states as well as small, it is non-alignment, not military alliances, that could be the means to peace.

For these reasons readers of this book may be interested in thinking more about this curious phenomenon – the emergence of a philosophy and an approach to world affairs by small states which saw their security and the security of great Powers in the creation of a just and peaceful international order as distinct from an order based on rival alliances and the balance of power.

Non-alignment is now the foreign policy of the majority of states in the contemporary world and, in particular, of those in the Third World. It is a general and active policy of involvement in world affairs. Although it was elaborated in the context of the Cold War, its validity and viability are not limited to the historical context in which it was first actively pursued. The reason is that its roots pre-date the Second World War and it has had a lively existence in the period of détente.

The founding fathers of non-alignment were Prime Minister Nehru of India and President Tito of Yugoslavia. It was they who took the leading role in crystallizing the policy and in calling the relevant conferences in the 'fifties and early 'sixties. They were joined by three other world figures from the developing countries. President Nasser of Egypt first met with Tito and Nehru to form a friendly triumvirate which met frequently to discuss world issues and then, as a movement got underway, they were accompanied by President Sukarno of Indonesia and President Nkrumah of Ghana. The origins of the movement can be traced back to discussions in the Congress Party of India in the inter-war period when it began to consider what the foreign policy stance of an independent India should be. In the post war world other countries were faced with similar problems. One of the early manifestations of the discussion of this issue was the Bandung meeting in 1955 which included not only the future non-aligned countries, but also some aligned countries such as the Philippines and the Chinese People's Republic. The movement proper, however, was not really founded until a preparatory meeting was held in Cairo and a full conference in Belgrade in 1961. In the meantime, Nehru, Tito and Nasser had, together and separately, developed the policy for their respective countries and implemented it. It is important, therefore, to bear in mind that the policy pre-dates and can be separated from the movement, particularly given the current vicissitudes of the latter.

THE 1961 DECLARATION

In 1961 the Belgrade conference gave rise to a 'Declaration of the Heads of State or Government of Non-aligned Countries'. In this Declaration the policy implications of non-alignment were set out as follows:

'The non-aligned countries represented at this Conference do not wish to form a new bloc and cannot be a bloc. They sincerely desire to co-operate with any Government which seeks to contribute to the strengthening of confidence and peace in the world.

The non-aligned countries wish to proceed in this manner all the more so as they are aware that peace and stability in the world depend, to a considerable extent, on the mutual relations of the Great Powers.

Aware of this, the participants of the Conference consider it a matter of principle that the Great Powers take more determined action for the solving of various problems by means of negotiations, displaying at the same time the necessary constructive approach and readiness for reaching solutions which will be mutually acceptable and useful for world peace.

The participants in the Conference consider that, under present conditions, the existence and the activities of non-aligned countries in the interests of peace are one of the more important factors for safeguarding world peace.

The participants in the Conference consider it essential that the non-aligned countries should participate in solving outstanding international issues concerning peace and security in the world as none of them can remain unaffected by or indifferent to these issues.

They consider that the further extensions of the non-committed area of the world constitutes the only possible and indispensable alternative to the policy of total division of the world into blocs, and intensification of Cold War policies. The non-aligned countries provide encouragement and support to all peoples fighting for their independence and equality'.

It is important to note from this Declaration that the non-aligned countries did not wish to become a bloc. They also stressed their willingness to co-operate with all countries whether from East or West in their search for peace. In the pursuit of peace and, also, in their desire to assist countries to achieve independence and equality, the non-aligned states asserted that they would play an active role and that they wished to participate in the world decision making system on these issues. In the course of the 1960s the non-aligned countries were active in the issues of independence and equality, especially in Southern Africa. They also began to be active in the United Nations on security issues as well as on development questions.

THE 1970 DECLARATION

Almost a decade after their Belgrade meeting the non-aligned Heads of State and Government met again and issued a further Declaration in 1970 called, 'The Lusaka Declaration of Peace, Independence, Development, Co-operation and Democratisation in International Relations'. The title of this Declaration points to the main values of the non-aligned movement. The movement looked to the United Nations as a forum in which they could pursue these aims and especially 'the fight against colonialism and racialism which are a negation of human equality and dignity, and the struggle for economic independence and mutual co-operation on a basis of equality and mutual benefit'. A further political statement of the non-aligned movement occurred at the end of a decade in which it had expanded in membership and heterogeneity, institutionalised itself and embraced an ever wider set of issues. In 1979, the Havana 'Political Declaration of the Sixth Conference of Heads of State and Government of the Non-aligned Countries' reiterated many of the principles of 1961 and 1970 including, after much discussion, the reassertion of the 'independence of non-aligned countries from great-Power or bloc rivalries and influences and opposition to participation in military pacts and alliances arising therefrom'.

The official policy of the movement made it quite clear that the non-aligned countries would have a dynamic and active foreign policy. It was in no way their intention to be passive or neutral in any traditional sense. They were determined, individually and collectively, to exercise their right to participate and to pass independent judgement on matters of concern to the world as a whole and, in particular, matters concerned with the East-West Cold War, with colonialism and race, with development and other related issues. However, in determining to act independently in a non-aligned manner in relation to world issues, the non-aligned countries were also aware that they would need to exercise internal independence. Therefore, they had to ensure that neither their political systems nor their economies were wholly dependent upon one source in ways which could prejudice their exercise of independent judgement.

NON-ALIGNMENT AND INDEPENDENCE

The non-aligned countries were not alone in being concerned with fostering the growth of national self-expression, with anti-colonialism, with fear of the consequences of the Cold War and with the need for development. These concerns were shared by all the newly-independent countries. However, the non-aligned countries felt that non-alignment rather than alignment was the best way to promote these values. Even those newly independent countries which were aligned, were usually aligned for 'local' reasons, not for reasons of the Cold War, which was the ostensible reason for alliances such as NATO, the Warsaw Pact, SEATO and CENTO. Pakistan, for example, looked to SEATO and CENTO for support in its struggle with India rather than seeing its role in those alliances primarily in terms of the Cold War. SEATO and CENTO were thus characterised and fatally flawed by differences of opinion between the great Powers - Britain, France and the United States - and the local Powers, about the purpose of the alliance.

The non-aligned stressed their independence in the resolution of their own specific domestic problems. They maintained that every country had the right to solve its own problems in its own way. They acknowledged candidly that many states in the movement had not succeeded in resolving their domestic problems and, indeed, that many of them were still flawed by both ideological and practical defects in the sense of internal exploitation. Moreover, they also freely acknowledged that there were regrettable disputes between members of the movement itself. However, whatever the flaws in their domestic politics and no matter how bitter the conflicts within the movement, they shared a sense of fellow feeling and self-respect after the experience of colonialism. Non-alignment is an integral component of this self-respect. One only needs to read Frantz Fanon's The Wretched of the Earth to understand why this was so.

One of the historic reasons for the growth of non-alignment as a policy was to safeguard the independence of newly independent countries. This was why Nehru, in particular, sought to ameliorate the Cold War which threatened to engulf the newly independent world. He reasoned that independence would be of little use if the world were to be destroyed in a nuclear holocaust. At the same time, however, each individual country had its own security problems. Nehru, Tito, Nasser and their colleagues believed that a policy of non-alignment enabled them both to solve their specific security problems by joining a wider movement and at the same time to deal with the general world security problem which was exemplified by the East-West conflict. Nehru argued most strongly that security came from policies and not from armies. Non-aligned political intervention in the East-West context to reduce the threat of nuclear war and to overcome the tensions of the Cold War would lead to a change in the system of power politics then pertaining between East and West. A happier relationship would ensue which would safeguard the security of the newly independent countries. However, not too much should be made of the Cold War as a source of non-alignment. It is quite likely that most of the newly independent states would have chosen something like non-alignment anyway. One has only to read the injunctions of George Washington to the newly independent United States in which he urged that the United States should not get involved in entangling alliances, to realise that some form of non-alignment or political independence is a phenomenon likely to characterise the foreign policy

72

of any newly independent state. The Cold War made this
tendency stronger. However, as time went by and as the
intensity of the Cold War began to decrease with the
development of detente, the non-aligned movement began to
turn its attention more to the question of development and,
in particular, to economic development. Non-aligned philosophy emphasised the notion of self-reliance, not only in
political matters but also in economic relationships. This
was not to deny the need for trade or for the transfer of
resources from the North to the South, but it was a stress
on the need for a practical policy to generate a reasonable
degree of self-reliance and, thereby, to gain self-respect.
It has led more recently, not only to the North-South debate
on the New International Economic Order, but also to an
increase in South-South economic ties.

It is important to bear in mind that the non-aligned
did not consider themselves to be a bloc, but a movement
which shared values and a common experience. This sense
of fellow feeling helped them to think together despite
ideological differences. As North-South issues became more
important many members of the non-aligned movement were
also members of the Group of 77, which grew out of the
first meeting of UNCTAD in 1964 and which did have a common
policy. The non-aligned movement, however, was more flexible
and less closed to others. Moreover, it was not only
concerned with economic issues. The determination to be
a movement rather than a bloc was reflected in the fact
that the non-aligned movement did not have a permanent
Secretariat at first and resisted any suggestion of
institutionalisation. However, during the 1970s the need
was felt to develop a limited degree of institutionalisation.

NON-ALIGNED INSTITUTIONS

At present the Heads of State and Government of the non-
aligned countries meet in a summit conference every
three years. The last summit conference was in New Delhi
in 1983. In the year preceding the summit conference
there is usually a preparatory meeting of foreign ministers.
In the intervening period there are also a large number
of ad hoc and regular meetings. The host of the previous
summit meeting usually acts as Chairman of the movement,
so that at the present time it is Prime Minister Gandhi
of India. The Chairman is the spokesman for the movement
as a whole and the contact man and person responsible
for ensuring continuity. It is also his duty to supervise

the implemention of the decisions, resolutions and directives of the summit conference and other meetings. His delegation at the United Nations has an important function because it is there and, to a lesser extent in Geneva, that the non-aligned movement maintains permanent contact.

A Co-ordinating Bureau which now consists of some one third of the membership helps the Chairman to carry out his functions. Its meetings are usually held in New York with the participation of the UN ambassadors of the respective countries. However, any member of the movement is entitled to participate in any meeting on an equal basis. The non-aligned movement does not take binding decisions with a legal force, nor is it bound by a treaty. Nevertheless, it has a strong set of shared working habits which give it a surprising degree of cohesion. Decisions are usually effective because they are not taken on a majority basis but by consensus. If there is a consensus then implementation of the decision is not likely to create insurmountable difficulties. A consensus was defined at the 1979 Havana summit meeting as, 'A certain indefinable quality hard to express in words although we all know instinctively what it means.... Consensus is both a process and a final compromise formula..' Reservations to the consensus are allowed but 'cannot block or veto a consensus'. In order to promote consensus members of the non-aligned movement try, on the whole, to avoid open confrontation and they feel obliged to discuss disputes, even if they are party to them and they are contentious. Indeed, there is much informal discussion before a meeting is held and frequent use is made of open-ended working groups. Thus issues are aired in a participatory and open manner and this tends, even when there is a basic disagreement, at least to facilitate understanding. Surprisingly often, it also leads to consensus.

The non-aligned movement can perhaps be described as having an independent approach to decision making rather than a policy. It is not concerned with seeking a compromise position between those in conflict, but in getting to the roots of the problem through an independent approach to the issues. It is issues rather than countries which matter. Given this spirit of independence there is often difficulty in reaching agreement when faced by particular issues in which its members have different self-interests. However, its decision making processes, an awareness of the world community interests and a sense of fellow feeling, often enable it to arrive at consensus. Members are fully aware that without consensus the influence of the movement is greatly weakened.

THE HAVANA SUMMIT IN 1979 - SOME CONTROVERSIAL ISSUES

Non-alignment is basically concerned with high politics, that is with political and security questions. Economic, social and cultural questions are of concern insofar as they enter into the realm of high politics. In order to be non-aligned a state must be independent in all domains. This does not connote autarky, but merely the assurance that there is no exclusive relationship with one or a group of outside states in any particular area. However, this is to view non-alignment in terms of the world as a whole. It can, also, be a policy in a particular set of relationships. Thus, India has historically been non-aligned in the East-West Cold War, but it is certainly aligned in the Sino-Soviet relationship. On the other hand Indonesia is non-aligned in both the East-West relationship and the Sino-Soviet relationship. Thus non-alignment exists at two levels: at the world level and as a particular policy option for a state with regard to a specific issue.

Some of the differences between the two levels came to the fore at the meeting at Havana. On the world level there was a dispute between Cuba and Yugoslavia about the role of the Soviet Union. The Cubans argued that the Soviet Union had helped the non-aligned countries on anti-colonial issues and that it was not responsible for the underdevelopment of the South. The Cubans, therefore, recommended that the Soviet Union be given general support by the non-aligned movement. Yugoslavia replied that any general commitment to one side was a negation of the idea of non-alignment. Non-aligned countries still needed to play a major role in the context of the East-West struggle. Nuclear war, after all, could still negate all the victories over colonialism and destroy the possibilities for economic development of the Third World. The Yugoslav view predominated and Castro, while Chairman of the movement, respected it.

The role of the Soviet Union was not the only contentious issue at Havana. Membership of the movement and, in particular, that of Egypt, Kampuchea and the Polisario Front all gave rise to heated debate, but in each case the question was fudged. In 1961 at Cairo and Belgrade the following criteria were laid down for membership of the non-aligned movement:

1 That the State in question should have an independent policy based on the notion of coexistence with other States with different political and social systems and that it should be non-aligned in its foreign policy or follow a trend in favour of such a non-aligned policy.

2 That the State in question should give consistent support to movements of national independence.

3 That the State in question should not be a member of a military alliance which was functioning in the context of Great Power conflicts.

4 That if the State in question had a bilateral military alliance with a Great Power, or was participating in a regional defence pact, it was not doing so in the context of Great Power conflicts but for other reasons.

5 If the State in question leased military bases to a foreign Power then it was not doing so in a Great Power context.

These criteria have been greatly attenuated in the last twenty years. To an increasing degree any state which claims that it is non-aligned will be accepted into the movement. However, China is not a member, nor are the NATO and Warsaw Treaty Organisation states.

At first the non-aligned movement was primarily concerned with creating conditions for peaceful coexistence between East and West and for dismantling colonialism. More recently the promotion of economic development in the Third World has been the dominant concern. As President Nyerere of Tanzania has put it, 'the real and urgent threat to the independence of almost all non-aligned states thus comes not from the military, but from the economic powers of the big states. It is poverty which constitutes our greatest danger ....' Moreover, the 1970 Lusaka Declaration pointed to the 'structural weakness in the present economic order' and suggested that 'the development of the developing countries is a benefit in the whole world' and the major concern of the 1970s. In the economic area the non-aligned movement does have an action programme and this has led to some merging between the non-aligned movement and aligned

Third World countries. Another aspect of policy that the
non-aligned have stressed is their fight against racism,
which includes aspects of Zionism. More recently they
have sought to improve world communications, both in the
media in the form of a new information order, and in
transport.

HAS NON-ALIGNMENT A FUTURE?

The non-alignment movement has some substantial successes
to its credit. It helped to keep the Cold War out of significant portions of the Third World, not least, Africa and
the Indian Ocean. It had a calming effect on East-West
tensions. It has pushed a reluctant world to take a stand
on anti-colonialism and, in particular, a stand against
the white racist regimes in Southern Africa. It has
contributed to a growing awareness of the need for a New
International Economic Order. It has given a measure of
international legitimacy to the notion of independence.
While it has not led to the abandonment of coercive politics,
it has contributed to their amelioration. Yet it is not
without its serious difficulties as it enters its third
decade as a movement.

Prime Minister Nehru accepted the idea of the Belgrade
Conference in 1961 with great reluctance. He preferred
a highly informal but influential grouping and feared that
the essence of non-alignment would be lost if the movement
became institutionalised. Twenty years later his fears
have, to a significant extent, been justified. There now
appears to be virtually no control on membership as
internationally committed states of left and right join
the movement. The non-alignment movement is in danger of
changing into a Third World pressure group with a consequent
complete change of character. The 'Third World' character
of the movement has been emphasised by the commitment to
economic development and the New International Economic
Order, on the one hand, and the failure to recruit developed
neutral countries with a non-aligned potential, on the other.
The victory of the Yugoslav thesis over the Cuban analysis
has given the movement a respite in which to decide whether
it is 'non-aligned' or 'Third World'. The current crisis
in détente highlights the need for a non-aligned input into
East-West relations. However, heterogeneity in membership
remains, reducing the degree of fellow feeling necessary
for the reaching of consensus. As consensus is more difficult to achieve, so the effectiveness of the movement
declines. It risks becoming a trans-continental Third World

talking shop which can safely be ignored by the rest of the world. Heterogeneity of membership also leads to more institutionalisation in order to co-ordinate the growing numbers. These two factors can cause impotence.

Nehru's fears of institutionalisation of the movement were not justified in the 1960s, but the 1970s saw an increasing degree of formality in the movement. The non-aligned movement is not yet a bloc, but as it becomes more of a Third World pressure group it begins more and more to participate on the same basis as others in bloc politics or power politics, which in its infancy it sought to overcome. Nehru envisaged a loose concert of concerned states that would 'stay in touch' in a flexible way rather than an institutionalised caucus of some one hundred states. Institutionalisation encourages group politics within the movement and the techniques of parliamentary diplomacy. This is a far cry from the special character of decision making evident in the late 'fifties and early 'sixties, which was based on a frank, free and fearless discussion of issues. The debate concentrated on the issues untrammelled by the exigencies of multilateral diplomacy. It could be fast and furious, but it was dominated by a shared sense of concern. It was what made the non-aligned movement different, efficient and valuable. It remains to be seen whether the respite won at Havana will ensure that despite heterogeneity of membership and of views and despite institutionalisation, this vital element in the non-aligned movement can survive. Otherwise, the non-aligned movement will lose its legitimacy in world affairs.

The New Delhi Summit in 1983 revealed an awareness of the problems and a determination of the Indian government, the new Chairman, to do something about it. But the task is difficult, for the movement has lost its way even if the policy remains both valid and necessary. Perhaps Mrs. Gandhi will be able to revert to the flexibility of a loose concert of a few like-minded statesmen within the framework of the movement along the lines originally favoured by her father. In the meantime, after more than twenty years as a movement and a much longer period of gestation as a policy, non-alignment is at the crossroads. Will it remain non-aligned or will it gradually become a Third World movement merging with the Group of 77 on economic issues with a stronger action programme and a secretariat for economic issues? There is room for both, but they cannot be combined if the non-aligned movement is to continue to make its unique and necessary contribution to world peace.

The members of the non-aligned movement do not have a monopoly of a non-aligned policy. Sweden, for example, has followed a 'purer' non-aligned policy than many members of the movement itself – and to great effect and to the benefit of both Swedish and community interests. In the context of the Helsinki process, Yugoslavia and the European neutrals – Finland, Austria, Sweden and even Switzerland and Ireland – have played an invaluable role both in achieving the agreement on the Final Act in 1975 and in maintaining the process since in a difficult and dangerous political climate. Some of the European neutrals have taken the lead in seeking to overcome the North–South divide and to support the movement called for by the Brandt Commission. They are not non-aligned, but they do reveal a concerned independence in both the East–West and North–South dimensions. Is the torch of non-alignment being passed from the Third World to European states to play an active but supportive role in world affairs? A country such as Britain, if it followed a policy of concerned independence, could help to fulfil a vital role, whether it did so alone, or in loose association with like-minded European countries with the resources to make an impact. Later we examine the implications of such a role for Britain in the dual context of the problems to be faced – and especially the East–West and North–South relationships – and the interests of Britain and of the world community at large.

PART III
THE ROLE OF THE THIRD PARTY

The role of a third party as a facilitator or counsellor is not well understood because tradition has it that there is a judicial or arbitral function associated with it. What we have in mind is a supportive role that attaches no fault to any party and tries to help those concerned to work out a resolution satisfactory to all. It implies help in analysing relationships, clarifying motivations, sorting out values and costs – the kind of thing that parties find it difficult to do alone especially in a bargaining context. The role of the conventional international mediator has been different. He has usually sought to apply legal norms and arguments of history and on this basis to find compromises. These have often proved unacceptable to authorities who have responsibilities for those they represent.

We wish to argue that the third party, supportive, no-fault approach, is possible at the inter-state level no less than at others. The third party role can be enacted by a state through its foreign policies.

In this section we argue that alongside the ordinary processes of coercive politics there is an opportunity for more constructive policies. A 'middle Power' is in a position to promote this parallel approach or 'second track' to security and peace (Chapter Seven). We describe the orientation of foreign policy that is required and the third party role (Chapter Eight).

7 The second track

In the present confrontation between the USA and the USSR, the United States seems to be issuing a challenge: if the USSR is prepared to co-operate in meaningful arms control negotiations, then it can be assured of a generous response by the USA. If, on the other hand, there is no such co-operation and, on the contrary, further escalation in the arms race, the USSR can expect a massive response from the USA with which it could not compete.

These options have been labelled the 'two tracks'. Clearly they represent strategic policies that face in opposite directions - arms reduction and arms escalation. However, whichever the direction, the pre-occupation is with the single issue of strategies and arms. In this sense a more appropriate model is a single track - leading towards reduced arms in one direction and increased arms in the other.

The use of this terminology reflects a single-minded pre-occupation with defence and strategy. It is characteristic of defence departments and foreign offices, but, also, of people generally. CND and other 'disarmament' movements are similarly preoccupied with this single arms control track – though facing in the direction which is the opposite from that of governments and officials.

This exclusive pre-occupation with strategic issues is, in our view, at the heart of the arms control problem itself. The starting point we offer is the politically realistic assumption that, despite the dangers and the logical consequences of a nuclear confrontation, no great Power, neither the USA nor the USSR, will ever be diverted from its deterrent strategies and its desire for superiority, at least while there is fear of attack and a consequent felt need for defence. No amount of marching and protest by people and no amount of threat by governments will alter this political-psychological reality.

If we accept this proposition that arms will escalate at least until the perceived need for them is removed, then attention is focussed on the steps to be taken to remove fear of attack and to establish associative relationships as an accompanying and parallel approach to a policy of 'security' through arms.

It is this parallel approach which is our notion of the 'second track'. The politically realistic challenge that the USA and the USSR need to make is, if there is co-operation in measures to reduce tensions and to resolve problems in relationships, then there can be meaningful arms control. If, on the other hand, there is no such co-operation, then there will be a massive response in arms competition. The challenge is, in terms of this two track model, to move together along both tracks simultaneously in a common direction. As advances are made on the second track, the reduction of tensions, agreements will be possible in reducing reliance on the first track, security through threat.

It is our view that the current debate that is taking place in Britain and Western Europe generally about unilateral disarmament, NATO and related issues is misguided. It is as misguided as was the debate as to whether inner-city, rioting should be controlled by more or by less policing. The reality was that the levels of policing required depended on the creation of jobs, better housing and better education. These were not alternatives: both police and better social conditions were necessary. The issue was not more or less policing, nor was it policing versus social conditions. Rioting required both, the two were complementary.

So, also, in the case of the strategic situation the world over and of British foreign policy in particular; the deterrence-disarmament debate is not only unproductive and divisive, it also distracts attention from the positive policies that alone can lead to arms reductions. Our realistic starting point is to assume that other than 'comestic' arms control and disarmament are politically unrealistic: there will not be effective arms control, let alone unilateral or multilateral disarmament, at least until there is no further felt need for arms.

THE ACCOMPANYING TRACK

The second track approach does not imply the introduction of a competing or opposing approach. On the contrary, the proposition that there will not be disarmament until there is no longer a felt need for arms, implies that the means to security and the means to peace are not necessarily opposites, as those who make a frontal attack on arms strategies suggest. Coercive-based security and association-based peace making are both legitimate activities, compatible, mutually supportive and, probably, necessarily interdependent. The two approaches can be perceived as being in tandem, or on parallel tracks, conveying govern-ments towards the common goals of war avoidance and harmonious relationships.

This is a simple notion, but it needs to be spelled out because a tradition has emerged of confrontation between the two approaches. It is as difficult for 'doves' to appreciate that 'hawks' seek peace (even by processes that theoretically ensure war) as it is for 'hawks' to realise that 'doves' are being no less realistic in their positive approaches (even by processes that according to other theories ensure war). Furthermore, because it is governments that are responsible for strategic policies and because it is largely private people and organisations that are pressing for disarmament, government senses opposition and has to justify its policy and to resist the 'doves'. The two tracks have been perceived as going in opposite directions; in competition with one another. This effectively prevents government from pursuing the second track as an essential addition to its first track power strategies.

At the level of inter-state relations a similar antagonistic relationship is likely to develop within alliances if less powerful members perceive themselves as being the pawns or platforms to be used by one nuclear Power in its contest with the opposing one. For these political reasons it is in the interests of great Powers, not only to proceed, but to be seen to proceed along the second track as well as the first.

Because governments have traditionally concentrated on the first track, there is an imbalance between the two approaches. The United States of America has a national security council, a defence department and a foreign office designed primarily to pursue coercive strategies, not to mention secret organisations of several kinds with the same purposes. There are no government institutions for the purpose of analysing and resolving security problems outside this coercive framework. Even conflicts within or between countries in the United States sphere of influence are dealt with within a strategic framework. There is no department or section of government whose job it is to help resolve these problems. There is no 'national improved-relations' board. In some sections of the US Administration there is some understanding of the need for it, since Congress established a Peace Academy Commission precisely to examine the need for just such a body. Yet the imbalance is apparent. The situation is no different in the Soviet Union, Britain and elsewhere. What is required is to correct the imbalance, not to seek to remove one approach to security and peace in favour of another. Thus the 'second track' has to be not an attack on strategic policies but part of those policies, a central part of the activities of government. It is a part of defence strategy, a function of government no less than strategy and diplomacy is, but it is different from strategy and diplomacy in character and in professionalism.

The study of strategy is important in its own right. Given that there is a perceived need for defence by major states, given that there are and will be defence policies and weapons, then a discipline and professional expertise in relation to strategy is required. Furthermore, mistakes, miscalculations, misperceptions, escalations, self-perpetuating conditions, self-fulfilling prophesies and inexorable imperatives often bring policies into operation that seem logical in terms of capabilities, but are consequently dangerous and must be subject to professional analysis. Only informed and the most careful decision making can avoid accidents. However, one input into this strategic decision making must come from the experiences and perspectives of the 'second track', the examination of perceptions and motivations, the promotion of political

change and economic development in areas of strategic significance, unofficial communication and contact between parties,
interaction between practitioners and scholars and, most
importantly, the resolution of conflict within and between
the spheres of influence of the major states. The second
track can bear some of the weight of perceived threat and
of fear and can reduce the need for defence, perhaps to
the extent of reducing the rate of escalation and the margins
of error. It is in this sense that the defensive approach
and problem solving are complementary.

The defence track is the traditional one and well understood. We are here concerned to develop the positive second
track. It is more intellectually challenging. It is new,
having been called into existence by the irrelevance of
war as an instrument of control in the nuclear age and,
therefore, not understood, not explored, not financed.
It is not as yet a part of the 'political realist' tradition.

One of the difficulties that needs to be stressed is that
the first track is a built-in part of the role of states,
while the second track, insofar as it exists, has been
confined to private bodies and individual citizens. As
a result the second track has been perceived as being in
opposition, not merely to the first as indicated above,
but to the state itself. But, it is as much the role of
the state as is the first. It is as relevant for a state
to have a national peace council as a national defence
council and, in present circumstances, more relevant.
It is a role that must be assumed by the state if the first
track is to achieve its aims of security and peace.

This is not to say that there should be no private contribution. Just as the state mobilizes private industry for
strategic purposes, so the state needs to mobilize private
knowledge, research, insights, contacts and information
for peace purposes. Security and peace are national, indeed,
transnational and international concerns. It is the duty
of the states to mobilize the resources required to achieve
these goals. Communication at an official level is
frequently distorted, especially when bargaining positions
are adopted. The Partial Nuclear Test Ban Treaty commenced
as a confrontation between the USA, maintaining that on-
site inspection was required to differentiate between under-
ground tests and natural earth movements, and the Soviet
Union arguing that it was unnecessary. When scientists
from both sides met in Moscow in 1962, those from the USA
adopted the official US viewpoint while those from the Soviet
Academy of Sciences adopted the Soviet argument. It took

days before even these scientists could remove themselves from their political thinking. When they did and adopted a problem solving mode of discussion, there was agreement.

The same resistances are apparent in crisis situations. Although there is a 'hot line', the Afghan situation was not discussed on it. There was no information transmitted to governments through ordinary diplomatic means. It seems that the aim of removing an inflexible leader in Afghanistan and calming a volatile political situation which, besides having a humanitarian aspect, had a grave propensity for escalation, went wrong because of some unforeseen happenings; but there was no communication of intentions or events. Apparently, governments cannot formally admit mistakes or unpredicted failure through some unpredicted event. Nor are they allowed to do despite the unfortunate consequences not only for the local population, but also outsiders and, not least, the United States.

Experience has shown that a body of scholars, who in the normal course have means of communication with relevant authorities on an informal basis, can help in analysing the complexities of relationships as a whole and in communicating details of particular crisis situations as they emerge. Scholars are expendable: if they fail to arrive at understandings it does not matter. They can explore without pre-conditions and bargaining positions. However, their capabilities and role are confined. The task requires the logistics possessed by governments.

Our present interest and concern is the role of a middle Power, Britain in particular, in the promotion of such a second track. The second track notion applies directly to the policies of a state — both approaches are within the responsibilies of states. However, it is also a notion that applies to the whole of world society: there are some governments that are more prone and in a better position to pursue one track than the other. It is a psychological fact that parties to disputes, no matter how experienced and aware of dispute procedures, require a third party or facilitator in resolving their conflicts. For these reasons we are concerned with the role of a middle Power, such as Britain, in the promotion in world society and in particular states, of such a second track policy.

8 The third party role

If Britain were to become more independent as a foreign policy strategy in the nuclear world, it would be obligated to go further than the positive neutralism of the non-aligned, further than merely being in a position to make judgements on the perceived merits of cases. It would be obligated by its own interests to intervene as a third party, to prevent and to help to resolve disputes. As a Power with global interests or commitments and as a world trading country, this would be the main interest and the main motivation for an independent position. As a great military force, Britain had a power and a balancing role. As a less powerful state, yet one that still has widespread interests, its role must remain one that contributes to peaceful relations and to law and order, but by techniques that do not rest on military power.

This approach takes the debate out of the nuclear deterrent-unilateralist (nuclear) disarmament framework. The issue is not merely whether Britain as a middle Power should, in its own interests, opt out of alliances and independent deterrents. It is whether it can make a more effective contribution to its own security and to the security of the international community by itself enacting a 'third party role' or, alternatively, by providing the environment in which an appropriate semi-official organisation would enact such a role.

How, in practice, can a middle Power such as Britain act so as to perform this third party role? There are many areas of policy to which it can be relevant. First, there are the day-to-day decision making activities of government, policies that are made and followed in respect of situations as they emerge. Second, there are decisions in regard to alliances, associations and other institutional structures that may or may not be compatible with such a role. Third, there are domestic policies in the handling of internal conflicts. Fourth, there are opportunities for government to sponsor and to encourage non-government initiatives and activities that contribute to the exploration of problems and to improved communication on matters of foreign policy concern. Fifth, there are mass media activities that help to inform parties to disputes and their peoples of the facts and circumstances as seen by others. Finally, there are direct problem solving interventions that may be followed as part of foreign policy.

DAY-TO-DAY POLICIES

As we saw, the general worldwide trend to some form of non-alignment and a concerned independence suggests that states, other than the nuclear Powers, perceive their interests to be in making independent judgements on the merits of particular cases, outside alliances and commitments to follow particular policies. This is the behaviour of the least powerful states – they have no effective defence beyond a contribution to the creation of an international system that is based on some generally perceived element of reason and justice. This implies an analytical approach to situations.

It is tempting for a middle Power, especially one that was once labelled 'great', to endeavour to exercise influence more in accord with a traditional coercive politics approach to foreign policy. However, if such a middle Power were to enact a third party role, it would be required to respond with the 'objectivity' of a small Power. By 'objectivity' is meant a non-normative, supportive approach to all parties. This is not a matter of radical change. It is a matter of orientation. It is a matter of appreciating the points of view of all parties to a dispute. To take Iran as an example, whatever the subjective feelings about events, 'objectivity' and the opportunity to exercise any constructive influence required an understanding of those who were both opposing and supporting the Shah and Western economic and political influences, rather than the adoption of a foreign policy stance which reflected the power politics of the region and the conflict between the great Powers. The present situation in Kampuchea, brought about very largely by great Power competition which, in this case, involves China, requires an interpretation by a middle Power that stands apart from contemporary strategic positions and assesses the longer term consequences of the rivalry. Similarly, in relation to North-South arguments, a traditional policy tends to adopt a narrow state interest approach, which is short term in perspective and, therefore, probably not in its longer term interests. An independent policy suggests an orientation that is analytical and designed to promote a stable international society on which ultimately the well-being of the middle Power is dependent. It is the difference between an approach that endeavours to seek a gain through the exercise of coercive power and an approach that seeks solutions based on their merits. Middle Powers, in practice, no longer have the power to coerce. Nor can they acquire it through association with one of the great Powers. The third party role is an orientation that take political realities more into account, while at the same time taking advantage of the knowledge, experience and influence which many middle Powers retain, not least Britain. This would involve bringing to the third party role research and information sources, developed administration, trading links, political links through past associations, developed diplomatic networks, media influence and the like.

What this means in practice is not a great shift in policy orientation that would require an alternative administration, but a more informed, a more sophisticated, longer term approach to the day-to-day situations faced by governments. It is the kind of shift that is required by the changed circumstances of the international society in which middle Powers no longer join forces so as to exercise more control. In a nuclear world no combination of middle Powers can be effective in a coercive politics sense. Reality demands that power balancing and alliance structures are replaced by techniques that are more relevant to the circumstances and these are techniques which resolve problems rather than merely settle them by coercion. Although this is not a dramatic or revolutionary change in orientation, it is one that probably requires substantial changes in approach, in training, in administrative processes, in diplomatic behaviour and in processes of negotiation at the United

Nations and outside of it.

ALLIANCES

The need for independence in decision making and for an analytical assessment of cases on their merits, may not be compatible with formal alliance structures. The foreign policy of a middle Power enacting a third party role, following policies with the orientation outlined above, would be more in accord with a non-aligned posture. If membership of alliances were retained, there would clearly be severe strains imposed on alliance relationships if a party to the alliance were to be analytical in approach and to challenge interpretations of events and the policies associated with its alliance.

Earlier we argued that trends in world society were toward independence and away from alliances. It is a trend that commenced after the First World War in Europe. It remained a persistent trend after the Second World War and the rise of independence movements in the world outside Europe. While in British thinking alliances have been assumed to be the 'norm' within the broader concept of coercive politics, this does appear to be a parochial British experience rather than a universal one.

Britain should, perhaps, adjust itself to the possibility that independence will spread, especially under the pressures created by nuclear weapons. It could well be that the ultimate answer to the nuclear problem, the answer in the interests of the nuclear Powers no less than of others, is a world society that comprises states that are neutral, a world society comprising Austrias - neutral by treaty - with the great Powers supervising this neutrality in their own security interests. Strict rules, such as apply to Austria, about non-discrimination in trade and in all dealings, the absence of any foreign espionage or counter-espionage agents, the absence of any deliberate forms of intervention in domestic affairs - all carefully watched and supervised in the interests of international stability - could be the goal of the international system of states in the future. This is an alternative that needs to be contemplated - in the interests of all states, great and small.

It is difficult for British people to think about this issue. The long-standing tradition has been to be, not just a member of an alliance, but the leading member of one. Furthermore, the belief has been that British security has rested on its alliance policies.

This may no longer be the case. Britain does not have a decisive voice in NATO and can be led into stances and plans by decisions at military and political levels over which it has little influence. To what extent was the British government involved in the NATO decision to have a contingency plan to drop a nuclear bomb as a 'warning'? At what level was it consulted - military, ministerial, cabinet? Is it appropriate for the people of Britain and other Western Europe countries to be informed through a hearing in the United States Congress?

In any event, it is far from clear, as has already been argued, that in the nuclear age the traditional means of control of the international system - coercive politics, alliances and the balance of power - is relevant. There are strong theoretical and practical arguments which suggest that Britain's security in the nuclear age is better pursued by remaining outside any alliance structure, giving Britain the opportunity to exercise its influence in more fundamental ways. Britain cannot enact a power role, even within an alliance, and a power role is probably self-defeating and irrelevant. It can, nevertheless, have effective influence. As one Canadian commented during the UN Charter Conference of 1945, wisdom is not the monopoly of the great Powers and it is wisdom that is finally powerful.

DOMESTIC POLICIES

It is reasonable to argue that a fundamental requirement for defence against any foreign influence or control is domestic security and the internal loyalty of the nation itself. Moreover, there is a view that the need for defence often masks a lurking fear of the conditions of change that are developing within. Indeed, foreign adventures are probably stimulated to some degree by a political need to demand sacrifices and to extract loyalty in conditions in which it is lacking. It is conventional wisdom that this is finally self-defeating, because the increased costs of defence threaten internal security and loyalty even more. In such circumstances leadership, reluctant to admit to its own failures and that of the system, is tempted to hold to policies of competitive escalation in the hope of 'winning' this internal conflict. Politically it probably has no option. The final fling in defeat is pre-emptive aggression or some wild adventure. On this reasoning both sides in any dispute have an interest in helping the other to solve internal problems.

When asked whether large increases in defence expenditure would not be better spent on education, health, housing, industry and jobs, a British Minister recently argued that the defence of the realm had to take precedence over all other demands: what would be the value of education if the country were under foreign control? However, it could be that there is a greater probability of war and of foreign control as a result of massive expenditure on defence at the expense of the stability and cohesion of society.

Yet the problem is even wider than this. Conflict resolution and conflict avoidance in the sensitive and dangerous areas that border the two super Powers, depend to a large degree on the economic and political development of the countries concerned. This in turn depends on resources being made available from the developed states, which depends in turn on less expenditure on arms. Pressure groups prevent cuts in defence for this would cause unemploy-ment. The chain of events is clear: problems that threaten security relate to failures of domestic policies to promote the welfare of peoples in developed states. It was not for nothing that there was a major fight by smaller states at San Francisco in 1945 to have included in the United Nations Charter an obligation to maintain high levels of employment. The close connection between domestic and foreign policies needs to be acknowledged. Once acknowledged it could mean redistributions of resources away from defence expenditure as a means to greater security.

Domestic policies have a bearing on interpretations of foreign policies made abroad. Unless internal conflicts with minorities and with occupational groups are handled with the same problem solving approach, little credence will be given to interventions in disputes between minorities and foreign governments or conflicts between governments.

NON-GOVERNMENTAL ACTIVITIES

In a coercive politics framework, governments are the only effective actors in the inter-state arena. Once a more positive approach is adopted to foreign-policy making and relations between states, other agencies and persons have a part to play. In conditions in which suspicion clouds information, in which formal contacts are politically embarrassing, in which diplomacy is reserved and cautious, private citizens, academic institutions, trading corporations and others can open up channels of communication that are useful. The Pugwash conferences of scientists had, in the early 'sixties, an important exploratory function in relation to the test ban treaty. Contacts between academic institutions enable some insights that are not available otherwise. Between the Soviet Union and the West there are many such contacts, encouraged at times, discouraged at other times. As with diplomacy, these contacts are best between friendly countries and are sometimes frowned upon when pursued with 'enemies'. The reverse should be the case: the most important embassies need to be where the main job of improving relations has to be done. It is between countries that do not have good political relationships that academics need to operate. Again, this is a matter of orientation. Britain has experience in these matters through the British Council, but insufficient importance has perhaps been attached to its work.

It is clear that the mass media, especially radio and television, can be important sources of information and interpretation of foreign policies. In the coercive politics framework the media is employed as a propaganda agency; if a more positive approach is adopted then the media has a quite different function. Britain has had a long experience with overseas broadcasting and the reputation of an independent broadcasting corporation. If foreign policy were reorientated in the ways suggested above, the role of foreign broadcasting would be even more significant.

Only searching enquiry can lead to a reliable definition of the major problems being faced and to appropriate means for dealing with them. The independence movements after the last war, were not predicted. They have now been studied historically and theoretical explanations have been advanced to explain what took place. Similarly, scholars began to perceive the causes of the last war only when it was too late. At a conference at Bergen in Norway, held a few days before war broke out with Germany, Japanese scholars warned very explicitly that Japan had no option but to join the Axis Powers in an attempt to secure a co-prosperity sphere, having been deprived of access to markets in the Asian colonies of the European Powers during the Great Depression. The USA Secretary of State, Hull, subsequently offered an undertaking to the Japanese Ambassador that the USA would guarantee access to markets if Japan remained at peace with the West. It was wisdom too late. Bombers were already under orders to attack Pearl Harbor.

So it is with the present situation. Scholars are beginning to look at the underlying causes of East-West and North-South tensions. Not being content with explanations that are mere labels, such as 'aggression', 'expansion' and others, they are beginning to ask 'why' questions - why 'aggression'? Perhaps too late.

Clearly we need a predictive model or a set of variables to be examined, some means of anticipating 'aggressive' behaviour, fear and defensive responses, some basis on which to ask 'why'? questions. If the Soviet Union appears to the West to be aggressive and vice versa, why? Just for the sake of being aggressive? What are the variables to be taken into account? If we were to arrive at a predictive model we could arrive at an explanation and, therefore, at a reasoned policy. There are very many variables to be taken into account:- background preconditions such as structural factors that affect communications and inter-actions, cultural differences, differences in resource dependency, a sense of isolation and adverse discrimination, internal insecurities, the realisation that political systems are undergoing change, scarcities, unemployment, economic inequalities and social unrest, mass media that reinforce fears and anxieties. The first track is designed to exploit these fears and concerns and to 'win' in undermining the other side. It is likely finally to provoke a defensive response. The second track is designed to explain 'aggression', to determine the source of fears and concerns, to understand them, and to help remove those that are likely to lead to the threats that the first track is designed to withstand.

If such a model or set of variables were studied and examined at the policy level, less coercive and more constructive approaches might result. The Soviet Union has some real external and internal fears, some of which stem from past relations with the West. It is affronted by the West's self-imposed 'superior' technical and military role. It is frustrated in its endeavours to bring about political and social change where clearly this is being demanded by peoples living under unacceptable authorities. The United States is fearful because of its own internal and external insecurities. It is affronted by the claim that it should only have arms parity and it is frequently frustrated in its attempts to maintain the private enterprise system and political freedom within its own sphere of influence.

All this is predictable; but there are many subtle and

deeply felt fears and anxieties that do not come to the surface in ordinary bargaining and negotiating relationships. It is the stuff of which wars are made, the stuff that is discovered only after wars have ended. It is only by problem solving processes that what is hidden can be exposed. And unless the hidden can be exposed, policy cannot take it into account.

PROBLEM SOLVING INTERVENTIONS

Direct problem solving interventions are an important part of the role of a third party. Such interventions are well understood in relation to small groups and counselling practices. The application of these processes in the international field is more recent and not as well known. It is the role that the United Nations could have been expected to enact, but primarily because of the lack of relevant skills the UN has failed to perform this function. There are few cases of a direct third party role being enacted by a state or by an agency sponsored by a state. It could be that the state should not be directly involved any more than the Swiss Government is involved in the activities of the International Committee of the Red Cross. But even in this case the state has an important role to play in providing the base and the foreign policies that help to legitimise the work of the Red Cross.

There is at any one time a large number of internal and international lethal conflicts afflicting the world. There is a tendency for them to become mixed and to give rise to even more widespread violence and destruction. The potentiality for inter-community conflict has increased because of the existence, following decolonisation, of a large number of countries whose national unity is fragile and whose populations are divided by major social cleavages based upon languages, religion, ethnicity, class and tribal loyalty or a combination of these.

It was argued earlier that the two major nuclear Powers feel it necessary to have and to protect their respective spheres of influence. In the context of the East-West confrontation, regional conflicts present a ready means of infiltration into each other's spheres. The West, whether it likes it or not, has to protect regimes that are threatened with change, sometimes much-needed change, for fear of a pro-Soviet government and the East is in a similar position. Thus regional conflicts, which have their own indigenous origins, become a dangerous source of wider conflict.

There has been almost total failure of accepted traditional intermediary techniques to find peaceful solutions to more than a relatively small fraction of such lethal conflicts, communal and international. This failure has emphasised the theoretical, conceptual and practical shortcomings of conventional approaches to peacemaking. The record of failure is exemplified by this lack of success of efforts to prevent the short, but violent, struggle over the Ogaden that took place in 1978 between Ethiopia and Somalia and which had been foreseen almost from the date of Somali independence in 1960; and by the almost complete absence of even a token effort to find a peaceful solution to the long-standing conflict between Vietnam and Kampuchea. It is even more obvious in the case of intercommunal and other violent domestic conflicts, where potential peacemaking initiatives are additionally handicapped by difficulties of access to the parties, and by the twin problems of domestic jurisdiction and of implying some recognition of a party legally defined as 'insurgent'.

A wider variety of reasons have been advanced to account for the failure of efforts at peacemaking in intractable conflicts. Although these reasons ostensibly differ according to whether peacemaking is by great Powers or great statesmen, international or regional organisations, private foundations or private individuals, a pattern nonetheless emerges in the explanations advanced. First of all co-operating in any peacemaking effort is inevitably perceived by the parties to the conflict to involve dangers, risks and costs which they usually wish to avoid. Even the most powerless intermediary employing the most informal approach represents some pressure to agree or to abandon salient goals. Mere agreement to participate in a peacemaking initiative implies some obligation on the parties who are usually unwilling to jeopardise their freedom of action to preserve salient goals and interests. Hence, parties avoid intermediary initiatives unless these clearly suit their own purposes.

An obvious starting point for reform and innovation is to minimize the perceived risk of intermediary activity and to concentrate upon a type of intermediary that represents low levels of coercive potential and an absence of previous involvement in the conflict and interest in the final outcome. However, practical experience seems to show that powerless and disinterested intermediaries suffer from other handicaps. There is a record of activity by this type of intermediary – for example, religious organisations, private foundations and private individuals who are mutual friends of parties in conflict and who attempt to play a role in ending conflicts. Such intermediaries are especially active in intense domestic or transnational conflicts where efforts that are non-official have the advantage of not conferring any form of recognition of non-governmental parties. However, the success rate of such private mediation is far from encouraging. There is frequently an initial failure of private intermediaries even to 'penetrate the conflict' and obtain access to the parties. Absence of access to top leaders is constantly a problem in intercommunal and other intractable intra-national conflicts involving a non-recognised, insurgent party. The formal political incumbents in any intra-national conflict are usually reluctant for peacemaking approaches to be made to 'rebel' forces, even on humanitarian grounds. Allowing such an approach even by private bodies would imply some form of recognition of status entailing future obligations and the curtailing of the government's theoretical freedom of action in dealing with the situation. It is, also, sometimes physically impossible for an inter-mediary to make contact with insurgents. Insurgents may be highly fragmented and possess no generally recognised, central leadership to speak on behalf of the competing factions.

At the other social levels, the convention has developed of using low power, low interest intermediaries whose access is assured by their acknowledged professional competence as mediators. In many areas of society there exist professional mediators with established reputations, whose past records of success add to their credibility and expertise. Industrial conciliation organisations, mediation boards and individual conciliators exist in many countries and have frequently reached a position where their services are automatically invoked in the event of a serious conflict. Unfortunately, there currently exists no comparable process of professionalising and institutionalising the role of the intermediary to help in dealing with communal or inter-national conflicts.

Given the present unsatisfactory state of intermediary approaches at the level of international and intercommunal conflict, one source of helpful innovation undoubtedly lies in developments of peacemaking processes to deal with intense conflicts at other social levels ranging from the individual to the inter-organisational and industrial. These approaches share the common features of being both deliberately designed to minimise the perceived threat of intermediary activity to the parties in conflict or to their interests, and to enable parties to search for mutually satisfactory resolutions of their conflict. The basis of all the approaches to structured peacemaking is essentially non-directive and 'no-fault'. Increasingly, the relevant third parties are being referred to as 'facilitators', 'consultants' or 'zero-power mediators'. In addition, third parties of this type are also distinguished by their employment of a <u>problem solving</u> approach to finding a solution to conflicts.

This problem-solving approach stems from a number of assumptions about conflicts which are quite different from those characterising a <u>bargaining</u> approach. Non-directive, problem-solving approaches are now employed frequently in conflicts between individuals, in industrial settings, within and between organisations or departments and, occasionally, in potentially explosive confrontations between communal groups in urban environments.

No matter at what level problem solving approaches are employed, the underlying principles and the tactical aspects, such as the means used to initiate fruitful communication between adversaries and the role and functions of the third party, are the same. The aim is to find a low cost, widely supportable resolution to an existing conflict whether this is between individuals, groups or organisations. It can thus be regarded as a technique of <u>conflict management</u> rather than <u>conflict avoidance</u>. At all levels a third party is involved in some intermediary role providing a service to the conflicting parties and operating directly between the adversaries by setting up a tripartite structure to assist the peacemaking process. The basic objective is often to change the parties' evaluations of their own goals, of the range of realistic alternative means available to achieve those goals and of their own attitudes and behaviour towards their adversary. The parties in conflict are helped to search for a <u>resolution</u> as opposed to a <u>settlement</u> of that conflict, although the precise methods by which the exploration is conducted differ from level to level. 'Resolution', it should again be emphasised, implies that the self-supporting outcome is based upon the joint discovery of means whereby the parties can satisfactorily fulfil their goals without making the sacrifices demanded in a compromise settlement.

Experience confirms that a problem solving approach can be applied by a professional third party. What relevance does this have to a state, particularly a middle Power, acting as a third party? To what extent would the need to be supportive of all parties to disputes and to take an objective view of each conflict be incompatible with traditional relationships, viewpoints and values? To what extent would a positive third party role by a Western state be seen to be in the general Western interest, acceptable and supported? If so accepted, to what extent would it be suspect from an Eastern point of view? Should the state provide the necessary conditions for a non-governmental Red Cross type mediation organisation concerned with conflict resolution rather than enact this role itself? If the state adopts the role, what alterations in selection and training of foreign office personnel would be required? What would be the role at the UN? These and many related questions need to be examined.

There are several different levels of the East-West relationship at which a third party role is relevant. First, there is the direct relationship and negotiations between the two major Powers, such as SALT and related matters. Within a bargaining framework, where compromise is sought, there can be no useful outcome. No state can compromise on its security. In any event, the subject-matter does not lend itself to deals and compromises, for there can be no reliable and acceptable calculations of the relative value of different weapons. A third party role would be to avoid bargaining and negotiation. It would endeavour to promote discussion on motivations, fears, perceptions and intentions, to direct attention to costs and consequences and to provide opportunities for discussion of wider options, in the second track mode, designed to reduce the need for weapons.

Second, there are conflicts within the spheres of influence in which a third party can bring together the local factions with a view to promoting change and agreement within a problem solving context. The great Powers cannot perform this role directly; but both have a strategic interest in the resolution of the conflicts.

Third, there is the need to promote a dialogue at non-official or quasi-official levels, between officials and between scholars and others, to explore possible solutions to problems, to improve communications and clarify motivations and ideological commitments, to enable a feed-back of available knowledge into official decision making processes.

Such problem solving processes applied at the inter-state

101

level are not merely innovative. They represent a practical and conceptual switch beyond experience. Yet they are common place at other social levels. It is perhaps conceivable for such processes to be applied by the UN - if it possessed the relevant professionalism. It is less easy to conceive of a state enacting such a role.

The reason is not to be found in the nature of the state as such. The reason is essentially tradition - the tradition of coercive bargaining, the tradition that diplomacy is the 'art of the possible', the tradition that holds there is not a professional qualification relevant to conflict resolution. The type of training diplomats have and their selection are designed to produce what the Duncan report termed 'professional generalists'. At best this includes history, law and politics conceived within the classical tradition and philosophy that dwell upon security by deterrence rather than by association, upon the preservation of institutions and the status quo.

There appears to be no reason why diplomacy should not operate within a framework that attaches importance to the participation of relevant parties, to their interests and values, including values such as independence, participation, control, identity and ethnicity. However, diplomacy could operate in this way only if conducted by a state that was, and was seen to be, independent and concerned with the interests of the parties involved in conflict.

There are, therefore, two requirements. First, independence and freedom from any alliance constraints that prevent a no-fault, supportive approach to all parties concerned. Second, a professionalism in relation to problem solving processes.

The two are related. Now that Britain is not a great Power, it is in a position to switch out of a coercive political approach to foreign policy. Having done this, diplomatic approaches and techniques can alter.

A NEW DIPLOMACY

The diplomatic system was created at a time when communications made it necessary for responsible representatives to be positioned locally, to report, to take decisions and generally to act for and on behalf of the government represented. In present conditions of communication, press reporting and rapidity of travel, the diplomatic service has been reduced to a prestige role. Consular services remain functional in respect of trade, migration and such matters.

Various British reports on the foreign service (for example the 1969 Duncan and the 1977 Berrill Reports) would suggest that it now has this more limited function, yet the old establishments continue. In some capitals, for example Moscow, there is limited contact between diplomats and officials - the contacts are almost confined to those with other diplomats. This is also the case, though less conspicuously so, in the other main capitals. Contact with decision makers is rare.

There is a serious dysfunctional feature in traditional diplomacy. The strongest missions are with 'friends' and the weakest with 'unfriendly' governments. Diplomatic relations are reduced or severed in tension or conflict, just when they are most needed. So means are required to overcome this problem.

The question arises as to what type of service is appropriate to modern conditions. Ultimately, one could envisage an international system in which there is direct contact between governments, audio and visual, at most levels including in times of crisis, supplemented by frequent visits between officials and ministers as and when it is necessary for 'opposite numbers' to meet. The routine of trade representation, migration and such matters would be by consular officials, or, possibly, on a reciprocal basis so that each administration carried out these functions by direct communication with opposite numbers. The virtual elimination of diplomatic overseas posts can be anticipated.

A stage in this process would be to reduce the status of missions to almost a consular level and accredit one person to several governments in the same region, such a person remaining 'home based' and making regular visits as and when seemed desirable. Three or four such senior persons making short visits to posts under their supervision would probably be more effective and have more ready access than permanent ambassadors. Such a system would have other advantages of co-ordination. For example, the one ambassador accredited to several states in the same region could enact a useful role, especially if he were of such status to ensure ready access. There is, in the international system, too little co-ordinating activity of this type.

If this model were adopted there would be a Minister for

Foreign Affairs, and under him two under-secretaries, one in charge of administration and the home office and one in charge of overseas representation. The latter would have a small staff of professionals to carry out the supervising and co-ordinating functions overseas and the integrating function in policy making at home. There would be no or few positioned ambassadors or senior diplomatic staff.

This small professionally-trained co-ordination group would have as their primary function the monitoring of conflict situations in their regions, contact with parties to disputes, whether governmental or non-governmental, and the provision of problem solving opportunities with themselves as facilitators.

This model would be especially suited to a government that sought to enact an independent and positive role in world affairs, offering itself as a third party in disputes and actively participating in broader strategic and high policy issues of concern to the major states. This is the kind of middle Power role that seems to be required in the international system, the UN having failed to meet this need.

There are economies to be made, along with being more effective. The Duncan report gives relative costs of permanent missions as compared with visits by relevant people to meet their opposite numbers. Mostly 20-50 such visits for a week at a time can be made for the cost of maintaining an official at his diplomatic post abroad.

There is one note of caution to be sounded in describing the role of the third party. We have indicated that it is not within the role of the third party to make suggestions and to direct, but to be supportive and to open up options for consideration. If parties do not respond to a hint, then it has to be assumed that the proposal is not relevant. The role is to facilitate, to help find positive outcomes: the finding is for the parties. It follows that if there is a successful outcome, if there is agreement and the resolution of the conflict, then the heroes are the parties. It is they who have found the options that are possible and relevant. For the third party to play this 'low profile' role is particularly important when conflict involves political authorities. They are and must be seen to be in control: they seek and receive the help of professionals, but help only.

This raises some problems when the third party is a politician or public figure and may be one reason for the high failure rate of political interventions. The UN mediator suffers from the same disability. If a middle Power, such as Britain, were to enact such a role, it must be prepared to enact that role with discretion and without seeking credit that implied that the authorities in dispute were not masters of their own situation and of their own relationships. The heroes, we repeat, are the parties who find agreement.

A third party role should not be seen as a radical change in foreign policy, especially for a state such as Britain with its long experience of interventions. It is an adaptation to new conditions, conditions that make coercive settlements of disputes irrelevant and impracticable. Coercive responses are obvious and simple: if there is minority protest, suppress it. They are understood domestically and anticipated internationally. The whole tradition of diplomacy has developed in this context. Means of tackling relations which are conflictual that do not involve coercion are far more complex and require a different kind of professional training and experience. This is the extent of the change required – the pursuit of the national interest by other means.

PART IV
THE FUTURE

In this section we bring the study to a conclusion by suggesting a course of action. Chapter Nine reminds us of the domestic and foreign implications of an independent Britain. Chapter Ten concludes with the notion of 'Concerned Independence' and suggests the process of debate, consultation and decision.

9 Domestic and foreign implications

The eventual results of Britain adopting a supportive independent role will depend on how other governments and political groupings react to such a change. Success in the new role will depend upon the skill and flexibility with which it is played and upon the changed behaviour of others in response. We need to consider the range of likely reactions, and to anticipate probable responses. This Chapter lays out some of the ground for a debate about the problems which could be caused by the reactions of present allies and partners, adversaries and neutrals, customers and suppliers, debtors, creditors and spectators, to a major change in British external attitudes and behaviour. It begins by trying to identify those groupings whose interests are likely to be served by a switch to an independent role and those whose existing interests may be damaged.

Even a superficial consideration of the question, 'Who benefits and who gets hurt' clearly reveals that two broad categories are involved. One set of potential 'reactors' whose likely behaviour must be taken into account are those external governments and groupings (ranging from states such as the USA and the USSR to organisations such as Solidarity and collectivities such as Caribbean sugar producers) whose existing positions might be altered by Britain's decision to head for a genuine independence. Equally, however, we would need to consider those domestic elements within British society who either derive benefits from the existing structure of relationships or who might reasonably see that their interests would best be served by abandoning present alignments and exclusive relations. In both categories there will obviously be some overlap between losers and gainers. In many cases, governments and groupings will be affected, in their own eyes, both adversely and beneficially so that their reactions become a matter of balancing the help against the harm. Industrial organisations within Britain might fear that they will lose safe markets for one range of products, yet gain in other markets for an alternative range of goods. As with all political questions, the adoption of anything new involves 'swings and roundabouts' for those affected.

It is also important we recognise that this external/domestic distinction, so casually adopted, can obscure the fact that links between groupings, either adversely or beneficially affected, can and do cut across formal national boundaries. Britain is a highly 'penetrated' society, at the centre of innumerable transnational linkages, so that the adverse and beneficial effects of new policies cannot neatly be considered merely as those affecting external elements and those affecting domestic ones. Often the two are intimately linked.

Nonetheless, while bearing these links in mind, we will adhere to the traditional framework of external and internal reactions in this attempt to set up the debate. We will begin by considering possible responses among external 'reactors', both allies and rivals; trading and financial partners; the allies of adversaries and the adversaries of allies; recipients of aid and investment; suppliers of raw materials and investment funds; neutrals, non-aligned and spectators. Secondly, we will attempt to link these reactions to those of groups and organisations within Britain itself, ranging from those who derive substantial benefit from the status quo to those who are already pressing for change. The two essential questions that must be raised are firstly, how might external governments and groups react to an initial British decision to adopt the pattern of behaviour outlined in previous Chapters of this monograph; and, secondly, how would likely long term processes be regarded by others who are important in Britain's external

environment. We begin by concentrating upon the security
dimensions involved in such a decision and in the related
processes of adjustment.

ALLIES

At first glance it is likely that the United States
and Britain's NATO allies would, from a security point
of view, react most strongly to an independent Britain
and that the reaction would be disapproving at the least
and punitively negative at worst. However, this could
be a mistaken judgement. Firstly, it is wholly misleading
to talk of 'a United States reaction' to an independent
Britain. The USA is a pluralist society and different
groupings within the United States may have widely different
reactions to the idea of Britain's withdrawal from NATO
and the loss of US bases and facilities. It may, indeed,
be the case that the loss of the British 'aircraft carrier'
would be regarded as a serious cost within the Pentagon.
Opportunities for using the United Kingdom as a launching
site for missiles, or as a forward airbase for nuclear
armed planes (apart from communications and surveillance
facilities sited in Britain) may be so highly valued
that their loss would be resisted strenuously by the
US armed services. On the other hand, many of these
facilities are only important if US involvement in NATO
and the physical defence of Western Europe continue
at the same level after Britain takes up an independent
role. Moreover, if the adoption of such a role by Britain
were to reduce the perceived threat from the Soviet Union,
help to stabilise long term relations between Eastern
and Western Europe, lessen the perceived NATO threat
to the USSR, and begin to remove the need for a direct
US presence in Western Europe, then the medium term benefits
to the United States would become clear and substantial.
For the USA, deterrence does not rest on European bases.
Even the need for submarine facilities outside the
continental United States has diminished now that SLBMs
can reach the USSR from US waters. To the United States,
NATO may be becoming a cost in need of reconsideration.
The isolationist tradition in US foreign policy can emphasise
the possibility of a US defence strategy that no longer
requires globalist underpinnings. Hence, the medium
term benefits of a process whereby the United States
can be assisted in pulling back from an entangling and
potentially costly alliance may not be negligible, even
to US defence planners.

The Pentagon reaction is not, of course, the only one likely to affect the ultimate US orientation to an independent Britain. The psychological blow to a US administration of the loss of one of America's staunchest allies might be considerable (although the intensity of this blow might well be less than many British leaders anticipate). However, it is possible that such an 'agonising reappraisal' might not be wholly negative. The 'loss' of Britain might be regarded as getting rid of a liability rather than an asset. At the level of US public opinion, a more extreme reaction might be one of willingness to let Britain (and other Europeans unwilling to pay for their own defence) stew in their own juice. The medium term public reaction would thus be one of 'good riddance' to untrustworthy and penny-pinching allies who had battened on US goodwill, resources and protection for far too long. Such a feeling could well assist the White House to accept and adjust to changing circumstances in Europe. Many people in the United States could well be pleased to see the government returning to a limited form of isolationism, at least as far as Europe is concerned. All of this, however, is posited on the assumption that a move to make Britain independent is not an isolated act, but part of a process bringing about major changes in Europe as a whole.

What, then, might be the reactions of Britain's present European NATO allies to British adoption of a neutralist posture? Again, we have to consider a range of possible reactions. 'Withdrawal from NATO' can mean a wide variety of actions, beginning with the rejection of Cruise missile bases on national territory but continued membership of the alliance (Norway, Denmark) going on to some 'half-in/half-out' relationship with the formal alliance (France), and finishing with complete withdrawal from the alliance and abandonment of the commitment to collective defence. All military alliances imply costs of membership as well as benefits. These costs can be divided into costs of membership and costs of activation (i.e. fighting a war along with allies). In other words, merely being part of an alliance may well involve a pooling of resources and hence (possibly) cheaper defence and more effective deterrence, but it also involves loss of freedom of action and independent decision making, as well as the potential for being dragged into conflicts which are the concern of one (or some) of the members but not the others. This lesson was pointed up by the Cuban Missile Crisis in 1962, and not lost on the European members of NATO at that time. Hence with regard to

Britain's presence in or absence from NATO the question has to be asked; what are the costs and benefits to other NATO countries of Britain's membership (especially in the light of Britain's current strong support for the present US hard-line policy towards the Soviet Union)?

To some degree, the answer to this last question is linked with that of continuing US involvement in the defence of Western Europe. Apart from the 55,000 men of BAOR and RAF units stationed in Germany, and its naval and nuclear roles, Britain's major role in Western defence is to provide a staging post through which American assistance could reach Western Europe; an unsinkable (although not indestructible) aircraft carrier for US strike aircraft operating in a forward-base role outside the continental United States; a platform for possible medium range missile launchings, a communications and surveillance centre, a base for the safe naval shepherding of US resources to Western Europe, in the event of some crisis or a non-nuclear replay of the Second World War. Against this must be set two major costs of British membership of NATO. The first is the risk that Britain will become involved in some military adventure in pursuit of solely British interests of remote importance to other NATO members, such as the building of 'Fortress Falklands', thus running the risk of weakening the alliance against its main perceived adversary. Since Britain's withdrawal from 'East of Suez' and the abandonment of the country's pretensions in the Middle East and Sub-Saharan Africa, this must be a diminishing risk to other NATO members, although the Falkland Island crisis, Hong Kong, Gibraltar and the like, show that the possibility has far from completely disappeared.

Secondly, NATO members have to contend with the cost of being in an imbalanced alliance, where three of the members possess, in the last resort, an independent nuclear option not open to others. One cost of Britain's independent nuclear deterrent to the other non-nuclear members of the alliance is the fact that they can never be certain about the circumstances in which a British Government might choose to use its nuclear weapons. For the United States and France, the dilemma is that they are tied into an alliance in which two members can, in some last resort, use nuclear weapons which are not under their ultimate control. The question, therefore, becomes one of whether non-nuclear or nuclear NATO members would regard the cutting of alliance ties with a nuclear Britain as a net gain or a net loss, particularly in the cutting of alliance ties with a nuclear Britain as a net gain or a net loss, especially in view of the concern about nuclear weapons and US nuclear policy currently affecting Western European countries. Paradoxically, Western Europe countries might well be glad to cut defensive commitments with a nuclear Britain, even if part of Britain's becoming independent might be renunciation of such weapons as part of an 'independent' British defence policy. European NATO reactions to an independent Britain would partly depend upon whether both they and the US government felt it necessary and beneficial to reconstruct an integrated defence system without British participation. Three scenarios might be plausibly postulated. On British withdrawal:

(1) The United States remains committed to the defence of Western Europe and a refurbished NATO emerges in which Britain's roles are transferred to other NATO members.

(2) US commitment declines as American interests switch to other areas of the world and US deterrence becomes 'home based', both in waters around the US itself and in continental USA. The Western European countries perceive themselves confronting a continuing Soviet threat and produce a much more costly integrated defence system which matches Soviet conventional strength and perhaps produces a western European 'bee-sting' nuclear deterrent. With such a scenario, East-West European tensions might increase initially, (especially with West German involvement in control of nuclear weapons), but relations could eventually stabilize. Western Europe would no longer be involved in a global confrontation with the Soviet Union and the United States.

(3) US commitment declines as in (2) and other Western European Governments begin to reconsider the whole nature of their defence postures and policies and the threat posed by the Soviet Union and its allies. There might, for example, be stronger efforts to establish a European nuclear free zone, or an end to blocs and alliances in the region. A start might be made with some form of MBFR no longer complicated by the tying of US strategic forces to those of Western Europe and the process continue with further efforts to remove or manage potential sources of conflict within Europe,

including the Soviet Union itself. In this last process, the kind of independent yet outward looking Britain we advocate could play a major role.

There are, of course, many imponderables in such speculative scenarios. However, they make clear that the possible results of an independent Britain range from an effort to reconstruct what presently exists to a radical transformation of the structures of European-wide security. This forms a useful starting point for informed consideration of present British options. West German reaction to no longer having a nuclear Britain as an ally will depend upon whether the West German government sees Britain's move for independence as a threat to its immediate military security or as a new opportunity to explore the implications of Ostpolitik more fully. Similarly, all other European members of NATO might find Britain's choice an opportunity for reconsidering whether their chances of long term security and survival are best sustained by the maintenance of the present system of mutual, nuclear backed threat or by efforts to produce new structures and, more important, new processes by which conflicts within Europe can be faced and perhaps resolved. There are growing indications that some Western Europe governments are beginning to question their dependence upon US strategic and political decisions affecting Europe and the world. They might even welcome a process which begins to de-couple European regional problems from US global pre-occupations.

We should again emphasise that it is misleading to talk about 'West German perceptions' or 'Italian options', on the assumption that some unified national calculus of costs and benefits can be constructed for each of Britain's present NATO allies. Groups within each of the member countries will have their interests bene-ficially or adversely affected by Britain taking up an independent option, and by the working out of any of the scenarios outlined above, or some variant thereof. Apart from the sheer inertial factors which make the continuation of any existing policy an easier option than the elaboration and implementation of a radical change, vested interests gather round the continuation of any status quo, whether concerned with security or prosperity. Yet, independence, the establishment of new, European-centred processes and structures need not imply a loss of role or position for military forces or national industries, merely a shift of emphasis and

and a rethinking of what might reasonably be accomplished, at what cost and with what benefits.

ADVERSARIES

Whatever the impact on her present allies of Britain's adopting some independent posture, the nature of the impact will be affected strongly by another set of factors – the likely reactions to such a move by Britain's present adversaries in Eastern Europe, especially the Soviet Union. To many people in Britain these reactions are not a matter for speculation, but a foregone conclusion. In this view, the only thing that has kept Western Europe free and independent for the last thirty years or more has been NATO and US nuclear deterrence. Abandon these and it will not be long before an expansionist Soviet Union is attempting to undermine Western defences. Using the threat of reality of military force it will seek to plant Communist rule firmly on the Atlantic, the North Sea and the Mediterranean. Hence, any move towards British withdrawal from the shield that has kept us all safe from Soviet depredations will inevitably encourage the Soviets to reconsider the balance of forces in Europe and to take up again an expansionist option in Europe as the risks of real defensive obstacles and an automatic US response diminish.

For anyone who does not share such Cold War certainties about Soviet expansionism and the effectiveness of deterrence, the question of Soviet reactions to an independent yet active Britain is more problematical. It may be that some elements in the Politburo and the Soviet Ministry of Defence – the hard-liners, the hawks, the ideologues, call them what you will – are likely to see Britain's defection from NATO as providing an opportunity to undermine the collective stance against the USSR or, to remove finally the traditional threat to the USSR emanating from Europe. On the other hand, those factions within the Kremlin and the state apparatus who remain committed to some version of peaceful co-existence whereby the USSR can benefit economically and technically from _détente_ with the West, might see Britain's move as an opportunity for pressing on with their own line of policy, and as a sign that the threat from the West is not as significant as has appeared recently and certainly not as serious as is undoubtedly being made out by hard-line rivals. In other words, an independent Britain might begin the process of calming Soviet fears.

The very act of announcing and then beginning to pursue an independent British line may change the perception of key Soviet decision makers, cause them to rethink their own range of best options for achieving stability and security, and provide a useful weapon in the factional struggles which exist within the Soviet power structure.

On the other hand, it seems more realistic to recognise the decline of Britain as an important international actor in the eyes of Soviet decision makers. It is unlikely that members of the Politburo will be much affected by the single act of Britain becoming independent and, in Soviet eyes, isolated. Nor is the Soviet Union likely to accept as credible and genuine an assumption by Britain that her new role might involve intermediary functions between the Soviet Union and other regimes. The Soviet Union hardly appears to see itself as in need of third party assistance in settling its quarrels and stabilising its relations with other countries. Moreover, the USSR might prove highly suspicious of an independent and positively active role for the UK in other parts of the world, no matter how disinterested. Particularly in the Third World, such activity is likely to be perceived as neo-imperialism by Soviet leaders of any generation. The Soviet Union sees itself as a great Power controlling and settling its environment in a traditional, power political fashion. Britain's unilateral action is thus unlikely to have much impact upon Soviet planning and decision making, and certainly by itself will not do much to modify any Soviet perception of threat arising from the continuation of a Western European-United States alignment.

However, if the British initiative is perceived to be, or actually begins to be, the first stage in a major European re-alignment, then the Soviet leaders are more likely to see a lessening of the perceived threat to their country. This could lead to a variety of Soviet responses to achieve long term improvements in Soviet security. The most immediate effect could be in the field of mutually beneficial disarmament, at the least in terms of a Euro-SALT and possibly of a European nuclear free zone. In the longer term, the Soviets might attempt to restructure their relations with Western Europe. At one extreme this could involve some form of continent-wide 'Finlandisation' or, more realistically, the Soviets could come to terms with a Europe which was no longer merely the forward base of the rival super Power. The crucial question is whether a unilateral move by Britain would be seen as that first step in some major change of European alignments, or as some eccentric individual action that would have no further effect on the basic structure of alignments in the region.

On the other hand, Soviet leaders might indeed perceive the British initiative as likely to bring about major changes in NATO, the Atlantic link and Western Europe as a whole, and they might consider that the costs and dangers in spreading instability far outweighed the lessening of any threat posed by the Western European allies. Uppermost in the minds of Soviet leaders could be the possible effects of an independent Britain (and a changing Western Europe) upon the countries of Eastern Europe and their relationship with the Soviet Union. Would the break up of the US/Western bloc (would even the defection of Britain as one member?) set an unwelcome precedent for the less co-operative states of the WTO in Soviet eyes?

Here again there is a need to consider another set of actors whose reactions would affect any radical change in British policy. Soviet reactions to the adoption of an independent role for Britain would undoubtedly depend, in turn, upon the anticipated and actual reactions of its allies and clients in Eastern Europe. What might the reaction of WTO countries be to a unilateral initiative perceived as a preliminary to a major West European re-alignment?

Much depends upon which East European country and regime is reacting. Britain's adoption of a unilateralist security posture and a withdrawal from NATO would undoubtedly have a major impact. This could encourage a number of East European regimes to consider strengthening trans-European links based upon a shared interest in not being entirely dominated by external super Powers and in reducing the danger of a nuclear war being fought across both Eastern and Western Europe. Even in countries where strict adherence to the Soviet alignment and its attendant patronage is the rule, an independent Britain might not be entirely without impact. The growing peace movement in East Germany, for example, might be able to use Britain's adoption of an independent position (and any subsequent effects on NATO structures and postures) as a weapon in its campaign to push the Honecker regime in the direction of support for discussion of arms reductions and the establishment of some form of military disengagement in Europe by the super Powers. This process could be particularly encouraged if it became plain that the adoption of an independent position by Britain (and reactions by other NATO governments) meant that East European regimes would find it more difficult to point to a threat from the West as a reason for continued escalation of military preparedness. Moreover, such an obvious lessening of the 'threat from the West' might also have a major 'destabilising' impact upon the East European societies themselves, and this again could be a major negative factor in any evaluation of a new British stance. It seems likely that the sense of being endangered has helped the East European regimes to justify, and peoples to accept, the constant need to be on their guard, to sacrifice standards of living and an increase of political freedoms and to give their support to regimes which defended them against external danger. Once such a sense of threat beings to be removed, the justification for low standards of living brought about by the need to pay for constant vigilance, vanishes. The results of this may be truly destabilising to regimes that have relied on the existence of a threat to national security to justify other policies and even their existence.

An independent British line might, therefore, strengthen peace movements and some government anti-escalation policies and might lead to considerable change within Eastern political alignments. It could also strengthen anti-Soviet tendencies in some East European countries and this, plus a perceived increase of 'instability' in the area (the usual expression employed by those governments frightened of any form of change in a status quo) could lead to negative Soviet reactions. While the Soviets might welcome the impact of Britain's unilateral independent role in bringing about a diminution of perceived threat in Western Europe, they might equally perceive that such a process could impose significant costs in terms of loss of control in Eastern Europe, plus a higher degree of uncertainty in their dealings with their WTO allies. The key question would, therefore, be whether the benefits brought by an ending of the US-linked NATO threat would clearly outweigh the costs and uncertainties arising in Eastern Europe.

A further element in deciding Soviet responses to an independent Britain would be Soviet evaluations of what impact Britain's new role might have in the world outside Europe. An independent role for Britain does not involve some withdrawal into isolation and traditional 'Little Englandism', but a more positive, out-going series of policies which could well involve greater British activity in regions where there exist serious problems affecting British long term interests. Naturally, the most immediate and important 'reactors' to a new British role in such areas would be the local regimes themselves.

To a large degree, Third World reactions belong more properly to our next section dealing with Britain's economic partners but there are political implications to Britain's adopting a positive political role in the world not tied closely to that of the United States or to other European countries. The image of Britain as a mere subservient client of the United States may fade and possibly other governments' receptivity to British ideas and initiatives will increase. In one sense, Britain would be exchanging a diminishing ability to influence US policies from within the Western alliance for a problematical but promising ability to influence other governments from a position of independence. However, withdrawal from NATO is likely to have less of an impact than Britain's role on trade and development questions. While Third World governments are likely to welcome in principle any change making a European nuclear conflict less likely, the chief effect on such a move by Britain will depend upon whether such processes result in a diminution of East-West rivalries in their particular regions, and whether a lessening of East-West tension might possibly release resources to help in the development of the 'South' as suggested in the Brandt Report. However, there might also be fears that, with the attention of major Powers switched from open confrontation in Europe, there might be greater, but no necessarily benevolent, attention directed towards the Third World.

However, there are more positive aspects of a new British role to be considered by Third World governments. Would regimes in countries such as Libya, Israel, Zimbabwe, Nigeria, Angola, Vietnam, see a new independent Britain as a major benefit or a major threat to their own longer term interests? Could Britain pursue a policy of enlightened long term self-interest in regions of the world where the level of British activity has been decreasing for the last twenty years? The answer would depend upon two sets of factors. The first is the skill with which Britain operated as a disinterested, impartial and useful third party in helping to resolve (rather than create) local problems and conflicts. The second is the degree to which Britain can alter current economic relations with Third World countries so that they are no longer seen as one-sided, exploitative, and designed to protect Britain's short term interests at the expense of everyone else. What, then, are the implications for an independent role for Britain as regards relationships with suppliers, customers, and traders, both actual and potential?

CUSTOMERS: SUPPLIERS AND CONSUMERS

Britain is a trading nation. Hence, one of the major questions that must be faced by advocates of a radical shift in Britain's external policies is the effect this will have upon Britain's trading position and the British economy as a whole. This has been one of the central issues at the heart of debates about Britain's entry into the European Communities. If we assume that Britain has loosened its ties with the Communities, helped to reform its structures or withdrawn completely, the possible impact of an unencumbered freely trading Britain on the British economy depends radically on other countries reactions to our adoption of such a policy and most particularly on the reactions of Britain's present economic partners, customers and suppliers.

Four main problems need to be considered. Firstly, if we break away from the Communities, what impact is this likely to have on our residual ability to buy and sell from our current range of economic partners in Western Europe? Does this depend on the degree to which mutually advantageous relationships could be arranged with EC members? Secondly, what new trading and economic links could usefully be developed with other customers and suppliers, thus ensuring that Britain can sell what it produces and obtain what it needs in terms of food, raw materials and manufactured goods from industrialising countries, perhaps in the Third World? Thirdly, and more specifically, what short term arrangements might an independent Britain need as regards fuel and energy supplies, and what longer term contribution might an independent Britain make to circumventing the anticipated global energy problem? Fourthly, and perhaps most importantly, which sections of British society – interest groups and economic institutions – would most likely be affected by a switch from Britain's current pattern of economic relations?

A great deal has been written about the possible damage that might ensue from a unilateral British withdrawal from the European Communities. The main disadvantages are thought to be losing Community markets for British exports. What much of the debate seems to have missed is that how advantageous or disastrous British withdrawal might be, would depend upon what terms might be negotiated for Britain's withdrawal. Crudely, the question is whether Britain needs Community markets more or less than Community exporters need the British market. It is by no means clear where the balance of advantage lies in this respect. It is true that something like 40% of British exports currently goes to Community customers, and that the potential European Community market for British goods and services amounts to some 214 million people, compared with a British market for Community suppliers of 55 million. However, the British market has, over the last nine years, become increasingly important to key sectors of the Community's manufacturing and food supplying industries, and the key issue is the extent to which Community suppliers would be willing to lose this market, even in its present depressed state. Obviously, the possible loss of a market taking 40% of British exports could not be contemplated with equanimity, even in the short run. However, both sides would incur damages. This should lead to negotiations about some continuing relations of mutual advantage to British and European customers, consumers and suppliers. In this respect Britain's trading deficit with the European Communities might prove to be a bargaining advantage, while the overall surplus due to oil exports might reinforce the advantage, given the Communities' dependence upon oil imports.

The main arguments about leaving, and to a lesser extent of loosening ties with, or seeking reform of the Communities, thus turn upon the nature of that leaving and the conditions of British withdrawal. Much of the current debate about Britain's continued membership avoids considering this question, and is carried on in terms of whether an economically independent Britain would be able to protect some ill defined economic interests on its own, away from membership of a large economic bloc. Many arguments echo the fears of the Chairman of the CBI's Europe Committee; 'On its own, Britain would count for little in the world and carry little weight in international trade and economic negotiations. Inevitably, our job prospects and living standards would be impaired.' (Statement at the CBI Conference 2 November 1981). There is, in this line of argument, no other 'natural' grouping for Britain to join other than the European Communities, an argument which, it could be pointed out, could with equal force be applied to Japan both now and in the 1950s. Against this, arguments are marshalled either against the direct financial costs to Britain of remaining part of the Communities, or against remaining part of a protectionist bloc whose pursuit of its own economic interests is damaging to the rest of the world, and particularly the Third World.

However, an economically independent Britain or one loosely tied to a structurally reformed Communities, should be able to seek alternative partners, customers and suppliers, and be able freely to establish mutually advantageous relationships in both immediate and longer terms. What new economic links might be open to a Britain no longer tied to the present Communities set-up? Where could the British sell what they produce and obtain what they need in terms of raw materials, and manufactured goods which characterise countries in earlier stages of industrialisation? Could an independent Britain fit into and encourage the establishment of a mutually productive New International Economic Order, involving East and West as well as North and South, while avoiding the grosser protectionist aspects of both the present European Communities and an autarkic Britain?

The answers again depend upon the stance adopted by Britain towards the sort of freer trade relations between North and South envisaged, for example, in the Brandt Report. If an independent Britain could take the lead in establishing economic ties with the Third World in which Third World countries were allowed to become suppliers, not merely of raw materials or semi-processed goods, but of 'second generation' industrial goods in return for high technology (British) goods tailored to Third World needs, then the kind of mutually beneficial economic growth that is the objective of Brandt's proposals could take place. Naturally, this would involve a willingness on the part of British governments and British industries to abandon the principle of protection for declining industries, and the practice of protecting individual industries except in the short term so as to allow an internal readjustment in the structure of the British economy. However, the longer term benefits of such restructuring of British industry would lie in an increase in the Third World's ability to pay for other goods and services which Britain could produce. In other words, an independent Britain could embark upon a policy of long term customer-creation, enabling Third World economies to grow by becoming suppliers of goods other than primary products to the United Kingdom. This might be less spectacular than attempting to sell to oil-rich countries such as Nigeria or the Gulf States (although the maintenance and enhancement of such relationships is by no means precluded for an economically independent Britain). However, the big advantage of a customer-creation strategy is that it would work with the aspirations and policy objectives of Third World peoples and governments, obtain the support of members of UNCTAD and similar Third World pressure groups, and help to enable Britain to fulfil other aspects of a policy of concerned independence.

In slightly different terms, such a strategy would enhance and build upon the complementarity of British and Third World economies rather than having to overcome the competitive nature of the economies of other advanced industrial countries such as those in the European Communities. The choice thus seems to lie between economic relations with those already doing what we do, who might buy British; and those who do what could be beneficial to us but who cannot, at least in the short run, afford the goods we can provide. In the longer term, the latter offer a larger and potentially more challenging market for high technology, skill-based industries.

Similar remarks might well apply to opportunities for British links with the economies of Eastern Europe, including the USSR. In many ways, the economies of Eastern European countries are complementary to that of Britain, and while the European Communities offer a market of 214 million potential customers, Eastern Europe without the USSR offers one of 112 million and with the Soviet Union included, the size increases to 377 million. One of the major reasons underlying the growth of détente during the early 1970s was the Soviet need for Western technology and for high technology goods. This need has hardly diminished even if détente has declined into the current state of renewed East-West tension and attempted partial embargoes. Soviet, Hungarian, Rumanian and Polish reactions to the availability of new British suppliers of needed goods and markets for East European produce are unlikely to be negative (although the short term reactions of the United States are unlikely to be enthusiastic). Moreover, the fact that such opportunities are offered by a Britain that has deliberately chosen to strike out in an independent direction and, whatever its resultant defence posture, is no longer tied to the NATO alliance and the US nuclear arsenal, is likely to facilitate the building up of British-East European trade links. Once again, such a course of action would necessitate changes in the internal structure of British industry and commerce so that it became orientated to providing appropriate goods for East European markets, but such adjustments are likely to be less far-reaching than those forced by a policy of economic autarky or competition with other high technology economies. (The success of the Finns in exploiting the opportunities of the Soviet market in high technology goods shows what is possible). Moreover, Britain's unique position as an oil supplier is likely, at least in the short term, to give a marked advantage in constructing advantageous economic links with Eastern Europe as it is in maintaining productive ones with the members of the European Communities.

Crucial reactions to such a radical change in current British policies lie within Britain as well as with Britain's external customers and suppliers (actual and potential). What are the likely reactions from industry, trade unions, consumers and other interest groups? The need for a major readjustment to the structure of the British economy that will be called for if Britain does adopt a policy of economic independence, may be costly and painful. They might therefore, be resisted, at least in the short run. The strength of the resistance can be gauged by the reaction to the long-standing argument that Britain withdraw from the Communities, and from the implication underlying many of these reactions that abandonment of present British economic policies involves the sacrifice of a large number of benefits in return for speculative advantages at some time in the future.

Much opposition to an abandonment or loosening of the Communities' connection obviously comes from those sectors of the British economy which already benefit from an existing relationship. (All appear to operate on the assumption, mentioned above, that withdrawal from the Communities and the adoption of an independent economic policy will automatically end such links). Thus, speakers at the 1981 Conference of the CBI were united in condemning the idea that Britain could withdraw from the Communities and used phrases such as 'unmitigated disaster' and a 'criminal folly' to describe such a suggestion. It should be noted that the opposition did not emanate solely from specific industrial interest groups, or from organisations such as the National Farmers Union, (NFU) (who might be expected to underplay the more obvious inanities of the Common Agricultural Policy) of the Milk

Marketing Board, but from officers of the CBI itself, and from regional representatives. For example, it was argued that something like 100,000 jobs in Wales (10 per cent of the labour force) were directly 'attributable' to the Communities' membership (although it was not stated unequivocally that these jobs would automatically be 'lost' if Britain withdrew). Similarly, the Chairman of the CBI Europe Committee argued that the Communities' market currently accounted for over $2\frac{1}{2}$ million jobs in Britain as a whole. Given that consumers in Britain are less well organised than producers in making their voice heard, it was not clear whether they would similarly regard leaving the Communities as an unmitigated disaster. It may be that British consumers would not be so dismissive (as Sir Richard Butler of the NFU) of the argument that buying all imports in the cheapest markets of the world would only (sic) reduce import prices by 8 to 10 per cent. On the other hand, they might regard 10 per cent higher prices as a reasonable price to pay for producing wine lakes and butter mountains. However, there are strong interests in Britain opposed to any major reorientation in Britain's external economic policy.

Considerable thought, therefore, needs to be directed to the question of who is likely to be hurt in the short run by the adoption of an independent outward-looking economic stance for Britain, and how short term costs of changing over from the present structure of economic relationships can be minimised. Who benefits from the existing structure of economic links, how much, and, what substitutes might be found in the longer term? Linked to this, however, is the likelihood of maintaining existing beneficial links, and the terms upon which such concrete policy moves as withdrawal from the European Communities might be managed. It would be a mistake to emphasise only the negative and costly aspects of any change. It is true that industries and producers interacting beneficially with the Communities may have their short term interests adversely affected by the severance or curtailment of those links, just as farmers may be adversely affected by the withdrawal of the Common Agricultural Policy umbrella. Depressed regions of the country may no longer benefit from the provision of aid from the Communities Social Fund, although this could be made up by British Government payments from funds switched out of Britain's net contribution to Community budgets. However, other industries and, certainly, consumers should benefit in the short term from an abandonment of the Communities' protectionism, as long as it is not replaced by a British version. In the longer term even those industries adversely affected by withdrawal from the Communities may find that other opportunities can be opened up in new areas and with new customers and suppliers. The balance is not necessarily a negative one in either the long or short term. Nor is it likely to be a clear-cut case of unambiguous benefits or costs. Some reactions will bring beneficial results to Britain's economy while others will bring about considerable costs both to the economy as a whole and to particular segments thereof. All that can be done to anticipate the likely balance is to consider as many factors as possible, together with the best possible estimates of what sort of economic outcome might result from Britain assuming an economically independent role. The table on pages 128-129 demonstrates one form that such an appraisal might take, although it is only an outline sketch of the necessary analytical operation.

CREDITORS, DEBTORS

There is, of course, another aspect of an economically independent Britain that must be considered, if the overall range of possible reactions determining the relative success and failure of such a policy change is to be analysed. Britain is not merely a trader and producer, but also a lender and a borrower and, while the role of sterling as a reserve currency has more or less ended, Britain ironically now finds itself in possession of a 'Petro-currency'. The economic and hence political consequences of Britain's adopting a posture of concerned independence would be very much affected by how countries holding their reserves in sterling, or governments investing in Britain or in receipt of investment funds from Britain, reacted to Britain leaving 'the West' and possibly 'Europe' and striking out on its own.

In many ways, the most difficult thing to do when analysing such reactions is to ignore the short term reactions of Britain's creditors, investors and debtors and attempt to discern the longer term course of events. Certainly the immediate results of any British re-alignment would be largely negative. International financial markets do not respond positively to uncertainty and change. Reactions from outside economic and financial forces on Britain itself might be severe. Short term effects on the exchange rate might be highly adverse, if the achievement of a more realistic level for sterling is

Reactions to an Economically Independent Britain

		Benign Scenarios	Malign Scenario
1	Trade relations with EC	Reciprocally beneficial arrangements made	Full Community trade barrier re-erected
2	Investment opportunities in/with Western Europe	Remain open	Close to Britain
3	Balance of trade with EC	Positive balance	Large negative balance
4	Alternative sources of low priced food & raw materials	Readily available	Few and fierce competition
5	Third World markets for British high technology goods	Available and growing	Closed and stagnant/ declining
6	Creation of customers in Third World	Highly successful	Little growth

128

Reactions to an Economically Independent Britain

	Benign Scenarios	Malign Scenarios
7 Eastern European markets for British goods	Considerable	Negligible
8 World trade as a whole	Expands	Contracts/stagnates
9 Exchange rate for 'sterling-as-petro-currency'	Declines re. major reserve currencies	Remains high or increases
10 Exchange rate fluctuations	Stable	Unstable
11 Defence costs	Decline in medium/long term	Increase
12 Readjustment of domestic economic infrastructure	Rapid, flexible transition	Slow, costly change
13	....	....

is regarded as adverse! (Undoubtedly inflation would be given an upward twist in the short run. However, in the long run a permanent devaluation of sterling might prove to be no bad thing). The trend among British financial institutions and businesses to invest abroad, which began with the removal of exchange control regulations, might accelerate unless some form of short term control on the outflow of capital investment was reintroduced. It is already considerable.

Would reactions continue to be adverse once the rest of the world had accepted Britain's new choice of role? Would outside investors regard Britain as a high-risk area, subject to chronic instabilities? Moreover, would British investors continue to feel it necessary to move funds abroad? If the answers to such questions are positive, then there would be no longer term financial advantages to off-set the short term stresses likely to hit the British economy immediately after an announcement of a major reorientation of British thinking and policy.

There really seems to be no reason for such a dire prediction. The relative attractiveness of Britain as a place for investment would depend upon the existence of a skilled workforce, a stable society and the anticipated gains from investing resources in Britain over a long period of time, and these gains will depend upon relative labour costs and government encouragement for the restructuring of British industry which, we have argued above, would be a major component of any adoption of a policy of political and economic independence. A more realistic exchange rate might even result in a major inflow of short term investment, while the possession of North Sea oil would enable the British economy, in the longer term, to invest in industrial restructuring appropriate to an independent economic role for the 1990s. There seem no convincing reasons for believing that, in the long run, the British economy will not remain as indebted to outside investors who thus develop an interest in the survival, the continuity and prosperity of the country as it is at present. Indeed, if the viability and political benefits of such a policy reveal themselves, the net result might be Britain becoming more indebted to outsiders as the century nears its end.

What about Britain's role as an investor and a creditor in its own right? There are two aspects of this which would prove important for a Britain adopting a policy of concerned independence; investment and aid. In the case of the former, the most serious cost of adopting an independent policy and leaving the European Communities' might, indeed, be the loss of investment opportunities within Western Europe, (and also losing the Communities sources of investment in Britain), although this will depend very much upon the terms of withdrawal (loosening or restructuring) negotiated with the Communities' members. This is not a negligible problem, as a major part of the outflow of funds after 1979 went to Europe, the remainder going to North America. However, apart from negative reactions to Britain from Western Europe, there is nothing in a policy of concerned independence to preclude Britain becoming a creditor to economies anywhere in the globe, unless it is decided to attempt to concentrate British investment funds within Britain, at least in the short term, in order to carry through the policy of restructuring the British economy in line with its role for the 1990s.

It is at this point we would argue that, in our view, the most constructive strategy for Britain as a future creditor would be a long term one, which ties in with the trade strategy of customer-creation mentioned above. This strategy would imply that British investment should deliberately be directed towards helping the Third World develop the capacity to buy British goods, investment and consumption goods, even at the cost of foregoing short run benefits of investing in high growth, high income areas of the world such as North America. While this might be a major short term disadvantage, the benefits from such a strategy as regards Third World Governments and the breaking down of North-South barriers have already been mentioned. Such an economic policy by Britain would follow the sort of economic trends demanded by the advocates of a New International Economic Order, provide Britain with markets in the medium and long term, and help Britain fulfil other aspects of the role of concerned independence.

Moreover, an investment policy aimed at long run customer-creation, in the countries of Africa or south-east Asia, for example, could be complemented by a major British aid effort. This should have the objective of fulfilling Britain's long term interests in British and global stability and prosperity by complementing Third World countries' objectives of political stability and rapid economic growth. Paradoxically, this raises the possibility that Britain might not carry its independence as far as withdrawing from OECD, but merely try to influence the latter's strategies of development in the direction of creating future customers. Alternatively, a <u>British</u> aid effort concentrated on a particular region of the Third World, and carried out in conjunction with the governments of that region, might prove to be the most beneficial initial tactic, although care should be taken to establish a set of economic relationships which are mutually satisfactory to donors and recipients so that charges of neo-imperial control are seen to be without foundation. The objectives of the policy should be to complement Britain's role as an active problem solver, and this can only be achieved if relationships developed are functional, mutually beneficial and 'open', in the sense that Third World regimes are free themselves to choose the most beneficial further arrangements, whether these benefit Britain or not. There can be no sense of political tying of advice, aid or investment.

If there is one theme running through this argument about future creditor policies of an independent Britain, it is that the strategies adopted should be aimed at serving British interests in the long rather than the immediate term, and that short term benefits should be sacrificed whenever these appear to conflict with longer term advantages which have to be planned, worked for and awaited. Thus, note could be taken of the changing trade and investment potential in Africa as regards the economy of South Africa compared to other African countries which have aligned themselves against white supremacy and <u>apartheid</u>. This changing balance has recently been emphasised by the growth of the Nigerian economy since the civil war and the expansion of oil production, but this case is merely the first of a number of potentially large markets in Africa which could rapidly downgrade the importance of South Africa to Britain, both relatively and absolutely. Apart from the moral repugnance of <u>apartheid</u>, a rational strategy for an independent Britain could indicate efforts to build up major links with economies in Africa, whether their regimes are radical or conservative, pro-Western or pro-Marxist. An independent Britain, no longer tied to the coat tails of re-awakened cold warriors would be in a unique position to establish functional links with such countries.

Such changes would have significant repercussions within the United Kingdom, for a downgrading of existing investment links with particular countries, and their severance in other cases, would seriously affect powerful interests in the City and elsewhere in Britain. However, we again return to the argument that costs have to be balanced against perceived opportunities and criticism muted by the presentation of a radical strategy for British-as-creditor which promises long term advantages derived from opportunities for growth and development. Vision is called for, rather than the caution of the international banking fraternity.

OTHER INDEPENDENTS

One final set of reactions which we might well consider when we are building 'what-if' scenarios is that of other independents and semi-independents. What might be the reaction of other middle-rank independents such as Sweden? How would Britain's assumption of the role of independence with a strong element of activism and helpful intervention in the world's problems be greeted by regional and inter-national organisations charged with the maintenance of peace, stability and development in various regions of the world?

The answer depends on whether Britain's new policy is seen as a single, unilateral change or as the beginning of a movement away from rigid blocs and exclusive alignments, both political and economic. It seems likely that, even in the former case, Britain's decision to leave NATO and the EC will be greeted with some warmth by other neutralist and non-aligned countries, even though there might be initial scepticism. However, acceptance of an independent Britain, might come rapidly if Britain could prove that concerned independence was compatible with and complementary to positive neutralism and did not make the foolish mistake of trying to become a 'leader' of some non-aligned grouping. If the British move was followed by further changes in the attitudes and policies displayed by other countries in both Western and Eastern Europe, (perhaps leading to a diminishing of tension and instability in the traditional centre of the Cold War) then the non-aligned, whose original <u>raison d'être</u> was to distance themselves from and mitigate the effects of such confrontations, could only respond with enthusiasm.

One specific grouping whose reactions would be of immediate moment is the Commonwealth, the third of the famous 'three overlapping circles' whose existence was vaunted by British policy makers during the 1950s and early 1960s. An independent role might well be compatible with continued British membership (not leadership) of the Commonwealth, which is always characterised as the most informal, flexible and undemanding of groupings. It is undoubtedly the case that Britain's detachment from Western Europe would be welcomed by Third World Commonwealth members, while a move out of NATO would not be regarded with hostility. It might also be, however, that Britain's assumption of a positive and active role in global, and inevitably Commonwealth, politics would be regarded with some suspicion, perhaps merely as an attempt to regain and even expand the old 'Head of the Commonwealth' role abandoned reluctantly by the British in the mid-1960s. Britain's success in persuading her Commonwealth partners that the new role was intended to be a functional and mutually beneficial one would depend upon her activities being obviously for the long term.

SPECTATORS

In much of this Chapter we have concentrated upon the results for Britain of 'going independent' and upon the likely reactions of a world that, at least in the short run, remains much as it is at present, with alignment unchanging and commitments stable. However, this is not necessarily the most likely scenario following a British unilateral declaration of independence. Almost every country and government in the world might be an interested spectator for such a new British role and of its effect on the regional and global structure of international politics.

The longer term question for such spectators is whether this British experiment appears, in any sense, a 'success' and worth emulating by countries in similar (or even widely different) circumstances. If Britain can provide a new model for successfully coping with the international environment in the late twentieth and early twenty-first centuries, then other countries in Europe may follow Britain's example in detaching themselves from increasingly dangerous and entangling alliances and from limiting and protectionist trading blocs, so that an increasing number of countries in Europe and the world become independent and non-aligned.

The argument here is simply that Britain's UDI may begin a process which radically changes the nature of regional and possibly global politics, quite apart from effecting changes in more immediate problems such as the local nuclear balance in Europe, or détente between

East and West in what Moscow describes as the 'central arena' of world politics. What might emerge could be a category (not 'group' or 'bloc' or 'alignment') of independent European states keenly interested in the stability of their region and yet not identified with either of the present alignments. Once Britain has adopted such a role, its potentialities might also be recognised and seized upon by France, Denmark, Rumania, Holland, Spain, Greece or even Poland, so that the number of European middle-rank independents could grow rapidly, bringing about a major change in regional politics.

The next stage of the process may well be both an increase in the activities of the members of this category of European independents either through individual initiatives or in a functionally co-ordinated fashion, and the growth of the trend towards independence in other regions of the world. To some degree, these two processes are inter-connected, for the adoption of the 'independence model' depends upon the actions of those first adopting it, making other countries capable also of becoming independent. For Latin American countries to contemplate independence realistically, a prior condition is the encouragement of economic growth and non-aligned policies by rich, industrialised independents themselves. The two processes are intimately linked.

Whatever the final pattern of international relations by the time we reach the twenty-first century, Britain may turn out to be the first fully committed and aligned country to adopt a policy of concerned independence, but there is nothing to indicate that it must necessarily be the last. Whether others adopt such a role will, however, depend very much upon the ability of the British to show that the role is a viable and worthwhile one, both in the sense that it fulfils the needs of the British and that it can be seen to have a beneficial effect on the world in which the British operate. The pay-offs of independence have to be shared and the benefits mutually beneficial to the independent and to others in the system.

CONCLUSION

The discussion in this Chapter is merely a starting point for an analysis of the implications of an independent role for Britain. For some people, even suggesting such a role may appear shocking, an abandonment of tried and tested means of keeping Britain free, independent and secure and a jump into the unknown fraught with uncertainties and dangers. However, we would argue that the changing world and the alterations within Britain mentioned at the beginning of this monograph make a serious consideration of some form of outward looking, activist, independence essential for Britain as the decade proceeds.

Earlier we argued that trends in world society were toward independence and away from alliances. It was a trend that was evident in Europe after the First World War which, after the Second World War, became universal. While British experience and political theory as interpreted by British thinkers has assumed alliances to be the norm within the broader concept of power politics, this is to take a parochial view. World trends are different.

Britain should, perhaps, adjust itself to the possibility that independence will spread, especially under the pressures created by nuclear weapons. It could well be that the ultimate answer to the nuclear problem, the answer in the interests of the nuclear Powers no less than of others, is a world society that comprises states that are neutral, a world society comprising Austrias, neutral by treaty, with the great Powers supervising this neutrality in their own security interests. Strict rules, such as apply to Austria, about non-discrimination in trade and in all dealings, the absence of any deliberate forms of intervention in domestic affairs – all carefully watched and supervised in the interests of international stability – could be the goal of the international system of states in the future. This is an alternative that needs to be contemplated – in the interests of all states, great and small.

Above all, however, we are not arguing that the adoption of a new external strategy for Britain will at once solve all of the country's current problems, nor that a policy of activist independence will be entirely without costs. The costs that are probable may also be substantial. Many of the benefits will be long term rather than immediate. A gradual moving away from the perils of super Power nuclear confrontation, arms races, or accidental nuclear war will inevitably be a slow, laborious business, while the process of building up institutions and mechanisms for resolving conflicts, like that over the Falklands/ Malvinas, will take decades rather than years. Informed discussion about the balance of advantage of Britain's posture and all alternatives, not just that of a concerned independence, is urgently called for. It should be clear

that we are firmly of the opinion that the balance of
advantage does lie in striking out into the unknown,
partly because the known is so periously self-defeating.
Despite the likely costs of such a course of action
we feel that the equally likely benefits are worth striving
for even if the attempt has to be continuous, long-drawn
out, and even, at times, painful.

10 Conclusions

Usually books about the interests and policies of countries are written from inside looking out. They focus on apparent national interests in the light of perceptions of the wider world environment. We have chosen the opposite perspective. We have drawn attention to the global situation and its dangers and, in this context, the interests of Britain and the role Britain might play in helping to reduce tensions among states, to solve problems of conflict and to bring about some degree of 'normality' and stability. We have done this because it seems to us that Britain, perhaps more than most countries, is so greatly affected by conditions in the rest of the world. Its national interest lies in managing and influencing these conditions to promote its own values in the context of both its own and community interests.

Generalizing, the problems of world society are two fold. They are problems associated with East–West relations and with North–South relations. However, there are, also, other pressing and grave problems. The majority of humanity is under-fed, a high proportion is oppressed. There are literally millions of persons who are refugees, deprived of valued relationships and of the necessary physical conditions for a tolerable life. The inequalities of welfare and opportunity within and between states are, in politically realistic terms, a threat to organised societies. However, we have not dwelt on these problems because they are symptoms of deeper ones. We have confined ourselves to the role Britain could play in East-West and North-South relations, for these over-shadow complex problems of political organisation and divert energies from them.

EAST-WEST RELATIONS

We have made many points in relation to East-West relations and here we would like to summarize them.

Both theory and practice have led us to the view that the emergence of internal problems within the political and economic life of great Powers is due to some degree to the costs of expansion and of the defence of spheres of influence. To some degree, also, the foreign policies of great Powers reflect disquiet within these states. Whether it be internal problems of political participation or internal problems of employment that are being experienced, causes are likely to be attributed by ruling elites, not to their types of system, but to external influences. In this way problems that arise out of the nature of the systems themselves can readily lead to international tensions, suspicions and defensive postures that are self-perpetuating and self-accumulative. It is for this reason that we have constantly asserted that it is in the national interests of rival states to assist each other in solving the internal problems experienced by each other, to help in carrying out adjustments, and not to take advantage of internal difficulties. This, we acknowledge, runs counter to conventional wisdom and traditional notions of power rivalries. Our justification for this departure from the traditional is that the world society is in a new situation. It is a nuclear world. In such a world, coercive politics and wars are no longer rational options in preserving and promoting the national interest.

Furthermore, internal problems not only affect relations between the powerful. They are externalised to the Third World. It is relatively easy for a great Power to export some of its unemployment, to justify and to promote change in others towards the forms and values of its own political system by whatever means, and to support inflexibility by unpopular regimes that would

change without that support. Throughout the world we
have situations of change that are being complicated
and not resolved by the intervention of rival Powers.
One oppressive regime replaces another. The basic problems
are not resolved. We would be prepared to argue that
both the main Powers in the present East-West struggle
are in favour of change and development in the Third
World. In the absence of their power rivalry these changes
could be planned and helped; but in the power rivalry
one side promotes and the other opposes, regardless
of the interests of the peoples concerned. In our view
it requires the intervention of a concerned independent
state to draw attention to common interests in change
and to facilitate change by co-operation. It only requires
one of these conflictual situations to get out of hand
and the two main rivals could find themselves in direct
conflict. It would be over a situation in which they
had no real direct interest and which, acting together,
they could have resolved.

This interaction between the East-West and North-South
problems is not sufficiently appreciated, in our view.
The two major rivals go to great lengths in creating
an overkill capacity as though the main source of conflict
were between them directly. The probability is that
there will be some triggering situation in the Third
World, relatively unimportant to the great Powers, that
brings them into conflict just because they have spheres
of influence and because there is this weaponry and sense
of tension that exists as a result of it.

Europe is caught between the two. A fuse lit in the
Third World leads directly to Europe where the arms
are stored in superabundance and about which the super
Powers talk blithely of a 'limited' nuclear war. In
self-defence Western Europe builds up its forces at great
expense to itself, yet it is not able to influence the
great Powers or in any way to determine its own strategic
future. In so doing it denies itself the opportunity
of giving that economic assistance to the Third World
which it is in its interests to give. There is not
really any conflict between the countries of Eastern
and Western Europe – all could live together and, indeed,
assist each other. Yet the countries in both spheres
are paying the price of the East-West rivalry.

We have pointed to a complicated and dangerous set
of relationships. We have made the point that they are
not intrinsically dangerous. They are dangerous because

140

of the way in which they are being handled. There are, inevitably, internal problems in the USA and USSR. There are, inevitably, internal Third World problems. These interact. The great Powers cannot themselves handle their own problems nor can they prevent each other trying to ease their own problems by exploiting the rest of the world. There are, however, solutions – but not within the abilities of those concerned, certainly not without the assistance of sympathetic third parties in the resolution of their problems.

THE NORTH-SOUTH CONFLICT

The political realities in world society are that there are economic structures and institutions that are clearly inequitable in their results. It is not the fault of any state nor is it the fault of multinational corporations. It is the fault of history and the way in which societies have evolved. As a consequence a problem is presented to the well-off people within states and the well-off states have a sense of insecurity just by reason of the fact that they know that basic needs and the demands of perceived justice are not being met and that this has political consequences. The problem cannot be resolved by rivalries, adversary debates and conflicts. The problem, being a systemic and historical one, has to be resolved deliberately, by co-operation and consultation, by analysis and by due consideration of future interests.

The resolution of the problem is being forced on the well-off, who would prefer to push it aside, by the fact that there has been a democratisation of decision making. This has come about by a wide access to means of violence. Terrorism, in all its forms – minority rebellion, military coups – are all instruments commonly applied. The monopoly of violence of the state no longer exists. Furthermore, those who now have access to the instruments of effective coercion have nothing to lose. Paternalism, feudalism, 'minority rights' mean little any more. The second best or palliative is no longer sufficient. The choice for so many in all countries is now between a full life and no life. Deterrent strategies and the sanctions backing law and order cannot cope with this condition. It applies at the individual level, at the inter-communal and at the international levels.

We would not claim that the whole problem of underdevelopment and injustice is a North-South one. On the contrary,

there are severe internal problems within the developing
countries that prevent them developing. Whether it is
because of the post-colonial regimes that were put into
power by the outgoing authorities, or whether it is
more fundamental than that, the fact remains that the
majority, the overwhelming majority of developing countries,
are ruled by non-legitimized and frequently inefficient
and corrupt governments. It is easy enough to blame
imperialism and multinational corporations; but given
strong, efficient, honest local authorities, these could
deal with any aspect of 'quasi-imperialist' behaviour.
It is this internal problem of developing countries that
invites in the East-West conflict. A third party could
bring all the parties, local and global together to ensure,
in consultation with peoples concerned, the necessary
changes which could give political stability.

The situation in South Africa depicts on a small scale
the world situation. It is no fault of the whites there
that they are in this situation. It is the fault of
discovery, trade, history, prejudice and a host of factors.
It is the result of colonialism, which in turn had deeper
causes. Fault is not relevant. What is relevant is
the present and the future. Whites in South Africa are
no more likely to give up privilege than privileged groups
in India or Britain, at least until the future costs
are clearly seen. Indeed, the future costs have to be
seen and so to be in a sufficiently short time scale
for them to be perceived by those concerned. Terrorism
and world opinion are probably necessary stimuli to costing.
In our view, one of the roles of a third party such as
Britain, would be to make clearer the costs of resistance
to needed change.

The Brandt Report has been helpful in that it has tried
to make clear the potential gains to the privileged
West of greater assistance to the undeveloped South.
Similar reports would be useful that deal with social
and political issues and the political consequences of
underprivilege. Again, a third party role would be to
stimulate such investigations and assessments.

North and South have clear common interests. The special
problems of each can be resolved only by their co-operation
in resolving their different problems. Britain has a
tremendous advantage: it has its imperial experience
and insights into the problems of development and it
has, more particularly, a quite unique relationship
with so many countries of the South. There is still

a residual good-will there that can be put to good advantage - but it is eroding rapidly because Britain has failed to enact a positive role.

PROBLEM SOLVING

This monograph has within it some most unconventional ideas, ideas that contradict conventional wisdom, that imply policies that are the reverse of those with which we are accustomed. In this concluding Chapter we, therefore, try the patience of our readers by restating some of what we have had to say - in a few sentences. The East-West and North-South conflict problems have within them the seeds of destruction. Change is inevitable. If it is change by violence it will be catastrophic and, in any event, will only substitute one coercive regime for another. There can be smooth and acceptable change by processes of consultation and participation. There are ways in which this can be done - which we call problem solving.

It is not enough to know that problem solving can work since its success may be due to good fortune. So that it can be used intelligently, a proper conceptual framework needs to be elaborated which will act as a guide for future policy in dealing with conflict in all social contexts and at all organisational levels. In short, problem solving is part of a coherent philosophy whose value lies in its empirical verification. It is not a question of what ought to be but of what is practical. Only an adequate theoretical conceptualisation and explanation can make it work effectively and reduce the likelihood of failure.

The problem solving approach acknowledges the hard reality of conflict, as did Machiavelli and Hobbes, but it is founded upon different premises which revolutionise the approach to conflict in many areas of social interaction including inter-state and inter-communal conflict. Problem solving is far from being yet another plea for goodwill, for peace-at-any-price or for peace-if-only-people-were-reasonable, rational and fair-minded.

Three broad approaches to the handling of conflict and change can be identified; the legal-moral or normative approach, the coercive negotiating or bargaining approach and the problem solving approach. Briefly the legal or moral approach seeks to handle conflict by applying to it a set of legal or moral norms. It is a useful way of approaching conflict when there is a basic consensus among the parties about those norms: the rules of the game are accepted by all and what is at stake is merely their applicability in a particular case. Such a method of handling conflict is often used when the conflict itself is functional to all parties as, for example, in the British electoral process in which only one party usually forms the Government. There is real conflict between the parties, but the rules for adjudicating that conflict are acceptable to winner and loser alike - although this looks as if it is beginning to change not just in Northern Ireland but, for different reasons, throughout the UK since the 1983 election.

However, when there is dissensus rather than consensus over the rules of the game then the normative approach is of little value. Either the norms are rejected as inappropriate by one or all of the parties or they have to be imposed. The Covenant of the League of Nations set out a method for handling disputes which it was assumed was self-evidently reasonable to all rational men. Those who thought otherwise were deemed to be wilfully deviant and could, therefore, rightfully be dragooned through collective security into following the rules. Unfortunately, what was reasonable and rational to the victors at Versailles was not self-evidently so to the vanquished or the revolutionary. Thus, as the inter-war period evolved, the normative method of approaching conflict was eclipsed by coercive negotiation and bargaining. Dissensus reigned and those who were best able to manipulate a variety of means of coercion struggled to impose their will despite or at the expense of the wishes of the weaker.

Coercive bargaining and negotiation is the currency in which the dynamics of social relations are reckoned in the 'realistic' approach. Conflict is seen as ubiquitous since it results from an inherent drive to dominate in man or in man-in-society. Since not all can dominate, social relations are an exercise in coercion between the dominators and the dominated. Conflict, therefore, can only be settled and not resolved. By conflict settle-ment is meant a situation in which the victor or a third party is able to impose a settlement on the vanquished or the contending parties respectively by coercion or the threat of coercion.

The problem solving approach reflects a very different conception of peace. We use the phrase conflict resolution to distinguish it from the conception of the 'realist', which has been termed conflict settlement. By conflict resolution is meant a situation in which <u>all</u> those concerned – no matter how respectable or deviant – establish acceptable relationships. Thus there is no need for coercion because when a conflict is resolved the situation is self-sustaining through the satisfaction of the parties concerned.

A 'zero sum' conflict is one in which the gains of one are necessarily the losses of the other. Parties to conflict often see their relationship in these terms. They look upon it as a situation of 'them or us' in which if 'they' get the whole or part, 'we' will get what is left. What is more, this diagnosis of the situation quickly gives rise to behaviour based on these premises. Thus the perception of conflict as being zero sum leads to behavioural patterns on that premise so that the conflict becomes zero sum in its effects. But is this the 'reality'?

Even those who espouse the 'realist' approach would accept that behaviour is not entirely predetermined. Scarcity may set a premium on certain values or possessions. It does not dictate the particular means of achieving goals nor the specific detailed characteristics of goals. Not only can means to particular ends change, but so can the ends themselves.

The problem solver argues that the nature of social relations is such that there is, in theory if not always immediately evident in practice, an infinite range of possible goals and possible means from which an actor can select. In practice of course, time scales, lack of knowledge, incremental factors, systemic factors and the nature of the environment limit perceptions of choice of possible goals and of means to attain them. There is always an element of scarcity since doing one thing implies not being able, thereby, to do another. It is necessary to choose, but any choice involves opportunity cost; that is, if it is decided to pursue one value, then the effort, time and resources necessary for the pursuit of this value may not be available for the pursuit of other values. The particular choice that is made reflects basic values, it reflects the information that is available and it is affected by all the factors, both objective and subjective, that go into the decision making process. However, most social actors try to maximise or at least to satisfy a large range of values. They also try to minimise the opportunity cost of the pursuit of one set of values, goals or material possessions in terms of other sets which are important to them. Quite clearly then variables dealing with information, with roles and with structure are important.

Because there is an infinite possible choice of means and ends it seems likely that there is a choice available which should be non-conflicting. In other words, each actor or group in a social system could, in theory, given time and perfect knowledge, light upon a particular selection which does not involve any incompatibilities with the choice of ends and means of other groups in the particular system. However, why should a particular group, having already invested a variety of resources in the pursuit of certain goals, give these up in order to arrive at this compatible position? Why should they turn the other cheek? Why should they adjust when other groups do not adjust, merely to avoid incompatibilities created as much by the choice of others as by their own?

The first answer to this conundrum is that if there is not a mutual adjustment process, then at least some unilateral adjustment will avoid the necessity of paying the costs of conflict.

But there is a second reason why inter-active adjustment is a realistic policy. Most of the basic goals which groups, governments or parties in a conflict are searching for are not in short supply. Let us examine four examples of this: security, development, identity and participation. Both East and West seem to have opted for a policy of the armed camp. This seems to be palpably self-defeating in the sense that it engenders an armed camp on the other side, and its cost in terms of other values is very high. However, security can also be achieved through ensuring others experience security. The more security one party experiences, the more others experience. There is a distinction between the traditional, but often self-defeating protective security against a threat, in which security is measured by arms and territory held, and a conception of environmental security where security grows out of an environment that is free from threat. The latter type of security is not something which is in short supply: it can be enjoyed by all. It is what we described above as security through association.

Development, too, is not in short supply. Development is a multifaceted notion with economic, social, political and cultural dimensions. There is an interdependence element which ensures that development in one region stimulates development in others. So, too, identity and recognition through participation is a much sought-after prize and not in short supply. A high degree of participation exists if there is a situation in which thre is consensus on the decision making process, if everybody plays within it that role which he feels to be appropriate. There is no formal legislation, such as the right to vote, that can give a sense of participation; it has to be linked to a particular individual or group in a particular system of transactions.

The fundamental aim of problem solving is to bring parties to disputes to an awareness that they are not in a zero sum situation; that their relationship need not be perceived in 'them and us' terms. What the problem solver is really trying to do is to take the self-defeating elements out of decision making. The aim is to maximise goals not at the expense of others, but in the context of others.

Supportive techniques are non-hierachically based, non-directive and non-judgemental in character. They do not emanate from some authority such as the UN Security Council and they do not involve any judgement as to the merits of a particular actor in a particular case. Moreover, they are not outcome-directed in the sense that they have a pre-ordained goal. Rather the role of the person or group using supportive techniques is to provide information; information about facts and differing perceptions and information drawn from theory.

Problem solving is difficult to grasp both because it is conceptually different from conventional assumptions and because in everyday language it is not distinguished from negotiating and bargaining. Thus there is a problem of nomenclature from the very beginning. What is meant by negotiating and bargaining is a relationship which is assumed to be zero sum and, therefore, highly likely to be coercive. Problem solving, on the other hand, is looking at outcomes from which all parties can potentially gain. We are now fortunate in having an adequate experience and an adequate theoretical literature to guide policy along such a course.

POLICY

The question arises as to how a problem solving approach can be incorporated within the policy of a government. We have taken a view that a prior condition is independence. This independence must be one oriented towards wider world interests, an independence motivated by a concern for the world environment.

Here again we have broken new ground. Concerned independence is an unprecedented approach to national interest. It is not isolation or autarky, on the contrary, it reflects the realisation that in a sustained set of relationships, self-interest includes components of community interest. It is an active policy designed to create supportive relationships in which problems faced by any or all can be sorted out by non-adversary processes, by analysis of the problems and by co-operative solutions.

Such an independence presupposes a strong consensus within the country. A country not at peace with itself cannot be at peace with the rest of the world, let alone make a positive contribution to difficulties experienced by others. This, in our view, was the weakness of the non-aligned movement. There was little internal cohesion within its members. Fortunately, despite its Northern Ireland problem, its inner-city problems, there is in Britain a strong consensus about democratic institutions, human rights, justice - though, let us face it, Britain has still a long way to go in bringing about an equitable and just society. It is an open society, there is diversity of view points, there is a high degree of freedom of expression and opportunity for expression. The liberal consensus provides the basis of the supportive approach that is fundamental to problem solving.

Independence does not mean going it alone. On the contrary, a country that is secure in its own value systems is free to act in concert with others with similar belief systems. A sense of security is the best guarantee of co-operation with others. It is true that Britain is experiencing a post-imperial crisis - it still seeks a role. Yet there is a basic confidence that enables it to be outgoing and to co-operate with others in the pursuit of common goals. Such co-operation does not mean any special relationships. It means working with others that are relevant in a particular dispute or situation. The partners will be different in different situations.

There is a danger that Britain, undergoing this post-imperial adjustment, will be tempted to contract out, to take a narrow view of its interests, to pursue trade and such strategic interests as a defensive posture. Indeed, two reports on the Foreign Office have recently reflected such a tendency. A concerned independence is contracting into world society, adjusting the diplomatic service and foreign policies accordingly. For Britain the starting point is probably the Commonwealth. Through it there exist links that stretch to most parts of world society. On the basis of these, further links can be forged with the East and with the South. To effect this a new type of diplomacy may be required, not the traditional accredited representative who, in practice, has little to do - at least in the political domain - but a professionally trained person who understands problem solving and who is 'accredited' to a number of states involved in a conflictual relationship.

A country that follows a policy of concerned independence is one that relies more on ideas than on weapons, more on professional training than on force. For this reason an internal infrastructure of higher education and research is essential. Britain, in contracting out, has tended to undervalue one of its most important resources, its educational system. A proposal similar to that for a United States Peace Academy would be a move in the right direction. Britain could well follow this lead that President Carter gave. Problem solving is an area that needs research, training and the building of a consensus.

We have tried to make it clear that we are not suggesting a policy of concerned independence as an alternative to all existing policies. We are not suggesting, for example, that independence implies necessarily unilateral disarmament. Nor are we suggesting that other states should necessarily alter fundamentally their strategic policies and co-operate in adopting problem solving approaches to their relationships to the exclusion of traditional defensive strategies. On the contrary, we are suggesting that there is no chance of effective arms control and disarmament until there is no longer a felt need for defence. This applies to Britain and to all other states. We are suggesting, however, that these traditional policies are, alone, inadequate and self-defeating. They need to be accompanied by more positive policies, a second and parallel track, that seeks to remove the causes of fear and the felt need for arms. The second track is not incompatible with defensive policies. Indeed, it is part of those policies. We would think that an energetic defence department following a hard line or realistic defence policy would include within its range deliberate attempts to resolve problems within the sphere of influence of its country and problems that could bring the country into conflict with others. The second track is not in competition with, still less is it in opposition to, traditional defence strategies.

We have not dealt particularly with wider economic and social issues. It is clear that the increasing expenditure by the Third World on arms, their increasing inability to find foreign exchange for necessary imports, even spares for tractors and machinery, the increasing political unrest that accompanies disappointed expectations, will lead to conflicts throughout large areas of world society. These could readily bring the great Powers into direct conflict. These more basic problems have to be sorted out both in the interests of the great Powers and in the interests of world peace. We have not gone into these because, as we see it, the immediate task is to focus attention on the dangers of East-West confrontation. If East and West can evolve some institutionalised means of co-operating to avoid conflict over Third World issues, then the way is more open for co-operation in resolving the problems themselves.

It is for this reason that we have suggested the need for improved means of communication, unofficial continuing seminars, means of monitoring crises and the establishment of some form of international mediation or facilitation service. There is a pressing need for the institutionalisation of problem solving processes at an official or an unofficial level, or a combination of the two along the lines of the Red Cross. It needs a relevant independent state to initiate this.

We have put forward the thesis that Britain should follow this approach, because we are working in Britain and we are aware of British interests and abilities. However, other countries are in a similar situation and have relevant experience and opportunities. Scandanavia, Mexico, Canada, Algeria, Australia and many others, could find that their interests were also in promoting a concerned independence for themselves and for others. We have argued that this is an extension of the non-aligned movement, it is part of the continuing trend from sovereignty to neutralism, to independence to non-alignment and to concerned independence. It is not a role uniquely for Britain, but Britain is in a unique position to promote it.

THE NEED FOR DISCUSSION

We have tried to list the political and economic implications for Britain and for others. These are far reaching and need to be analysed. Finally, decisions have to be made as to Britain's future role. There are no means of calculating gains and losses – the variables are far too complex. There has to be a judgement, an intuition, after debate and thought. For this reason we believe that the next step is to promote that debate and to organise discussion.

There are many parties and issues involved. First and foremost there is the USA–USSR relationship and consideration of the ways in which Britain could play a constructive role. There is the associated North–South relationship. Then there is the Western Europe alliance and the effects an altered British policy would have on the relationships and policies of Western European countries. There is the Commonwealth relationship and the consequences of such an altered role. Each of these would need to be worked through – first at informal levels and then at official levels.

There are, also, domestic interests to be considered. Here again there are very many parties and issues. There are those involved who have an interest in promoting activities, such as research, social development, environmental protection and others, who believe that the costs of the alliance structure and of British nuclear defence are too high in terms of these other goals. There are those who believe that the deterrence strategy is self-defeating. There are those who have an opposing view. There are trading interests and others to be explored.

In short, the means toward change is a process of consultation and discussion, exploratory and uninhibited by ideological, party political or other commitments and prejudices. This is not merely a means to an end, it is also an effective test as to whether the end of 'concerned independence' is desired, practical and beneficial in terms of the goals of national and international societies.

We have stressed the value of problem solving processes - analytical, exploratory and participatory. These same processes apply to the making of adjustments, for adjustments in policy necessarily provide perceived conflicts of interest. It is not for elected authorities alone to decide and to direct on issues of this complex kind even within the national system. In any case, many foreign governments and interest groups are involved. Nor is it for the public alone - it may not be fully informed. There is a need for debate and discussion. There is, at the same time, a need for early decisions. Debate and discussion sometimes are a means of delay.

High policy matters are traditionally regarded as the responsibility of elected authorities, acting on the advice of civil servants and with the persuasion of pressure groups. Parliamentary committees, in some instances, are in a position to seek advice and opinions and to make recommendations. There are, also, government sponsored commissions which make reports and recommendations on particular issues.

It is now arguable that the increased complexities and the interrelated nature of the problems we face - from defence to inner-city riots - have rendered inadequate or irrelevant these traditional decision making processes. In March 1982 the Secretary of State for Defence told the House of Commons and the public that only he and a few advisors have all the information on which to base a decision about weapons. Can we have confidence that he and Service Chiefs have reliable information and that they can reliably assess it and make major decisions about the nuclear deterrent? Furthermore, decision making processes are traditionally ad hoc. Separate policy areas, dealt with by separate departments and ministers, have been tied together to some degree by a political consensus; but the assumptions that underlie this consensus are now being challenged. These assumptions relate to the right of majorities and elites to govern, to the effectiveness of deterrence, to the practicalities of power balancing, to the limits of socialisation in multi-ethnic communities. There is, consequently, not even a philosophical framework that ties policies together.

The result of this condition can be a disintegrating society in which political decision making reverts to crude, why-they, ruling-ruled, informed-ignorant, powerful-powerless dichotomies. This is an adversary condition that gives rise to regimes that are increasingly authoritarian and repressive in domestic and foreign policies.

This is not to argue that those who are caught up in this process, whether they are in London, Washington, Moscow or elsewhere, wish to be so caught up. They are the victims of circumstances.

The creation of the Social Democratic Party was a reaction against the extremes of these dichotomies in decision making. Its adherents sought a middle position between extreme left and right and to re-establish the consensus of the 'fifties, 'sixties and early 'seventies. However, what is required is not a middle or moderate position on the left-right spectrum; but an advanced position on the non-analytical-analytical spectrum.

If it is correct that 'moderates' are in the same philosophical tradition as other ideologically-based political parties, if it is correct that politicians, civil servants, pressure groups, committees and commissions cannot find answers to problems because their framework is this same we-they, powerful-powerless philosophical one, then it follows that we need to break into an alternative philosophical approach that is analytical and problem solving.

It would seem relevant for the formal decision making process to be supplemented by non-governmentally sponsored commissions of inquiry into high policy issues, domestic and foreign. We suggest a process of consultation by a commission that takes hearings and receives evidence in public from anyone, in Britain or elsewhere, wishing to express views. This process has advantages over parliamentary debates and referenda which tend to be party political and adversary. In cases where complex subjects are being examined, in which there are, reasonably, greatly differing view-points, in which discussion and informed opinion are required, in which evidence is required from persons who have spent many years giving thought to the issues, a more analytical process is required. Evidence given before a selected group of commissioners and the deliberations of the commission during and after hearings could lead to the discovery of options and recommendations that would not emerge out of the ordinary processes of government proposal and parliamentary debate.

A commission of five or six persons could be established formally by parliament and report to it. Alternatively, there could be a commission established by private funding, outside government and its processes. The latter has some advantages. An official inquiry is suspect in an adversary party political system. The selection of commissioners and their terms of reference are believed to affect their findings. In any event, no government is bound by the findings of any inquiry, so there is no special advantage in having an official commission. An unofficial one that derives its authority from its professionalism, its processes and its openness could attract witnesses and evidence and produce recommendations that would be no less influential on government.

In short, the kind of adjustment to policy that we are suggesting is relevant to the nuclear age and it is too complex and too important to be left either to party politics or to mass movements. There is a need - an urgent need - for a professional inquiry, hopefully assisted by government and the public as all points of view and all knowledge need to be tapped. However, such a commission would have a useful and significant function even if no such assistance were forthcoming from government.

Such a commission would be required to examine all the proposals and possibilities that we have set out and others that would emerge - independent status, a third party role, freedom from alliances of all kinds, the sponsoring of continuing discussions between the opposing Powers and others. Intention and timing are interrelated. In an important way, intention can be an effective substitute for delivery when delivery is, for good reasons, delayed. There cannot be adjustment to policy overnight, there cannot be withdrawal from organisations without disruption, there cannot be the introduction of functional substitutes for constitutional ties. Timing and a programme can make possible that which would otherwise appear to be impossible. It would not be incompatible for a government to reorientate its foreign policies while still being a member of organisations which would in due course be irrelevant. It would be appropriate to begin to train a foreign office for a new role even before the old role was phased out. Indeed, the kind of adjustment that we have been discussing is an adjustment that will take place in any event in due course, perhaps in a crisis situation, perhaps through a change in government, perhaps through external or internal pressures such that we cannot now anticipate.

It is the processes of change that are important, the anticipation of change, so that there can be orderly change with consciously set purposes. Change that is sudden is usually a reaction against something. The positive goals are not then defined and may even be destroyed by the sudden change process. A considered, orderly change toward defined goals is the nature of conscious evolution.

Britain is faced with such an option. It can maintain the status quo in its external posture, despite the political realities of the nuclear age and be shifted from that posture by events. Or it can determine analytically its interests and those of the world society in which it exists and readjust its posture to meet the new circumstances. We have argued that there is a need for change, that Britain is capable of change and we have indicated the direction of this change. We have also suggested a process for change – problem solving. To get there we need to start with a popular commission – smooth, deliberate, consultative, open and informed to formulate the problem and to examine the evidence and the options. For our part we would recommend for Britain – in a world context – a concerned independence.